Warrio

The Way of Warriorhood

WARRIOR

The Way of Warriorhood

Bohdi Sanders, PhD

Updated and Revised Second Edition

Published by Kaizen Quest Publishing

Printed in the United States of America

Library of Congress Cataloging-in-Publication Data
Sanders, Bohdi, 1962-
Warrior: The Way of Warriorhood

ISBN – 978-1-937884-07-9

1. Martial Arts. 2. Self-Help. 3. Philosophy. I. Title

Acknowledgements

This book is dedicated to my two boys, Stephen and Colt. May you both become the warriors that I know you can be and that you know you should be. In the beginning, *Warrior: The Way of Warriorhood* started simply as a book that I had written to pass on to my sons in hope that they would take the wisdom in *Warrior: The Way of Warriorhood* to heart. If it hadn't been for my boys *Warrior: The Way of Warriorhood* would have never been written.

And, a very special and profound thanks to my lovely wife Tracey, for her editing expertise on this manuscript.

And finally, but certainly not least, I would like to thank the following individuals for their encouragement and endorsement of *Warrior: The Way of Warriorhood.*

Alain Buresse

Loren W. Christensen

Aaron Hoopes

Bob Orlando

Dr. Adam Weiss

Kevin Brett

Lawrence Kane

About the Author

Dr. Bohdi Sanders is a lifelong student of wisdom literature, the healing arts, and the martial arts. His studies led him to explore the wisdom behind natural health, naturopathy, herbs, Reiki, Qigong, meditation, and the power of the mind to heal the body and to make positive changes in one's life. These explorations led to him earning doctorate degrees in naturopathy and in natural health.

Dr. Sanders is also a Certified Personal Fitness Trainer, a Certified Specialist in Martial Arts Conditioning, a Certified Reiki Master, and a Certified Master of G-Jo Acupressure. He holds a black belt in Shotokan Karate and has studied various other martial arts for over 30 years. He has worked with young people for over 20 years and is endorsed to teach in five different subject areas. He is the author of:

- *Warrior Wisdom: Ageless Wisdom for the Modern Warrior*
- *Warrior: The Way of Warriorhood*
- *The Warrior Lifestyle: Making Your Life Extraordinary*
- *The Secrets of Worldly Wisdom*
- *Secrets of the Soul*
- *Wisdom of the Elders*
- *Modern Bushido: Living a Life of Excellence*

Dr. Sanders' books have received high praise and have won several national awards, including:

- The Indie Excellence Book Awards: 1st Place Winner 2010
- USA Book News Best Books of 2010: 1st Place Winner 2010
- IIMAA: Best Martial Arts Book of the Year 2011
- USA Martial Arts HOF: Literary Man of the Year 2011
- U. S. Martial Artist Association: Inspiration of the Year 2011
- U. S. Martial Arts Hall of Fame: Author of the Year 2011

www.TheWisdomWarrior.com

Endorsements for WARRIOR

In *Warrior: The Way of Warriorhood* quote number 54, Benjamin Franklin is quoted as saying, *"Reading makes a full man — Meditation makes a profound man."* Doctor Bohdi Sanders' insight on this saying is that, "You have to engage your mind and focus while you read... Meditate on the information... Don't just skim it, but... understand the principles behind what you are reading and be able to apply those principles to your life." Later he says that this applies to everything that you do, including learning the martial arts. "Do not let your mind wonder off to some other subject. Be in the moment. Focus on the Now. Don't just go through motions..."

As a practitioner of Zen, I believe that Dr. Sanders nails this quote so simply, yet so profoundly, that I think it should have been placed as *Warrior: The Way of Warriorhood* quote number 1, to function as a guide as to how to proceed through this most valuable book.

The wisdom sayings and the discussions herein are simplistic yet they are as meaty as a two-inch-thick porterhouse. I like simplicity in the martial arts. If you have read my books on the fighting arts, you know that I nag the reader as to the importance of keeping things uncomplicated. Real fighting is too fast, too furious, too heart rate accelerating, and too adrenaline pumping to employ complex techniques and concepts. I believe the same is true of one's personal philosophy. It has got to be simple and it has got to be pragmatic. Clearly, Doctor Bohdi Sanders believes this, too.

So don't race through this book as if you were reading a popular novel. "Meditate on the information," "be in the moment," and "...apply [the] principles to your life." Think about them and discuss them with your partner, your classmates, and with your students. Discuss them with friends outside of the martial arts too, as they apply to all facets of your life. Read this book, and then read it again and again and again.

Loren W. Christensen

Author of: *Fighter's Fact Book, Fighter's Fact Book 2, Solo Training, Solo Training 2, Speed Training,* and *Fighting Power*

Endorsements for WARRIOR

Warrior: The Way of Warriorhood is a book that modern day martial artists need. The knowledge that it offers to a new generation can be considered vital to the continuation of the true path of the warrior. Those who have spent their lives following this path understand that it is not about technique or physical ability. Instead it is about coming to terms with one's self. Once we realize that the most important battles are waged from within, then we are truly ready to learn.

However, *Warrior: The Way of Warriorhood* offers much more than that. It could also be described as a guidebook for the perfection of character, something that everyone, not only martial artists can benefit from. If more people were to understand the concepts of integrity, honor, and service towards others, the world would probably be a much nicer place to live.

Dr. Sanders has compiled a fantastic resource for warrior training. The format is wonderful. The book is made up of 170 quotes, with each one focusing upon an insightful bit of wisdom. The quotes range from Einstein to Japanese master swordsman Miyamoto Musashi and the unique commentaries of Dr. Sanders delve much deeper into the meanings of each quote. Some are simple to understand, such as; *"Warriors should never be thoughtless or absentminded,"* while others may require a more in-depth study, *"Though the wind blows, the mountain does not move."*

The depth of the book reflects Dr. Sanders own warrior training and it is an honor to be asked to contribute to the front matter of this book. I will surely be using it as a resource guide in my Zen Warrior training program.

Aaron Hoopes,

Founder of Zen Yoga and the Zen Warrior Training Program.
Author of: *Zen Yoga: A Path to Enlightenment through Breathing, Movement and Meditation, Perfecting Ourselves: Coordinating Body, Mind and Spirit, Breathe Smart: The Secret to Happiness, Health and Long Life,* and *Eat Smart: The Zen Anti-Diet.*

Endorsements for WARRIOR

Although I consider myself a full-time martial artist, I have never seen myself as a "warrior" (especially when our real warriors are those men and women out there that are fighting the enemies of our nation). That said, I find *Warrior: The Way of Warriorhood* by Bohdi Sanders an excellent and highly motivational, even inspirational book.

Serious martial arts study is as much mental as it is physical, and just as one cannot attain or appreciate martial skills without serious and constant practice, neither can one effectively control and rightly apply those acquired skills without some kind of wisdom. Studying and understanding the noble warrior's mind is, therefore, an excellent way to truly master one's martial skills, and Bohdi Sanders' book, *Warrior: The Way of Warriorhood* provides a very good way to gain that understanding.

Bob Orlando

Martial Artist and Author of: *Martial Arts America: A Western Approach to Eastern Arts*, and *Indonesian Fighting Fundamentals: The Brutal Arts of the Archipelago*.

Endorsements for WARRIOR

Honor, discipline, wisdom, and character building, all part of a martial artist's arsenal, that is what the reader gets from *Warrior: The Way of Warriorhood* and much, much more. I highly recommend *Warrior: The Way of Warriorhood* for anyone involved in the martial arts and even those of you who may be thinking of going into a particular style of martial art.

Warrior: The Way of Warriorhood is a book that I would strongly suggest that you read before, and after, your daily training in the dojo in order to get a complete education, and realize the true spirit of the martial arts. This book would be a great gift for anyone, regardless of whether or not they, or you, are even involved in the martial arts

Dr. Adam Weiss

Martial Artist, Black Belt and Author of: *The BackSmart Fitness Plan,* and *The AbSmart Fitness Plan.*

Endorsements for WARRIOR

Warrior: The Way of Warriorhood is actually much shorter than its 208 pages might lead you to believe, yet quite memorable nevertheless. While you could easily read the whole thing from cover to cover in a few hours, I believe that it is far better to savor the materials. Pick a page or two a day and spend some time absorbing what you have read.

While the individual quotations could easily stand alone, the author's succinct three to four paragraph commentaries add quite a lot to the experience, helping you digest the information and explore your own character as it relates to the topic. Whether you agree with the author's interpretations or not, all the sections are thought provoking. With a little "think time" many of them can be quite profound.

The quotations themselves are an interesting blend, eclectic and insightful. Some are from folks you'd generally associate with martial arts and/or bushido such as Gichin Funakoshi, Masaaki Hatsumi, Forrest Morgan, and Ed Parker, yet others such as Marcus Aurelius, Charlemagne, George Patton, Sitting Bull, Tecumseh, and George Washington not so much. Nevertheless, they are all on topic, making for a profound and provocative treatise.

This is by no means a "punch here, strike there" kind of book. It is, however, a thoughtful look into the philosophical side of the warrior arts, one that I've found well worth reading and contemplating upon.

Lawrence Kane

Author of: *Surviving Armed Assaults and Martial Arts Instruction*; co-author of: *The Way of Kata, The Way to Black Belt,* and *The Little Black Book of Violence.*

Endorsements for WARRIOR

This is the second in Bohdi's outstanding series on Warrior Wisdom. When I reviewed *Warrior Wisdom Vol. I*, I stated that the content is not limited just to warriors and martial artists. There are three challenges with acquiring wisdom as I see it: first, you must find wisdom and recognize it as such; second, you must interpret and internalize it, and third, you must put it into practice as part of your daily life. Bohdi has taken care of the first two issues. Once again he has assembled a montage of timeless wisdom that without the efforts of sages like Bohdi is at risk of being lost. There are always quips, quotes and salient points floating by us as we go about our lives. Bohdi has masterfully collected, identified for us and provided sound interpretations of the many valuable insights contained in this volume.

This is the type of book that you can read cover to cover, but you don't have to. Pick it up, flip to a random page, read it, discuss it with your spouse, kids, colleagues and think about how to apply it to your life! We always tell our children the cliché, "Make good choices..." as they leave for school each morning, hoping that somehow that trite phrase will make them a better, stronger person and keep them out of trouble. Good choices must have a basis is good learning. We must understand what is or is not a good choice, a good way to conduct our selves. We must understand what is a bad course of action and what choices lead to a stronger person with solid convictions based on tried and true maxims. Bohdi continues to provide us with those golden nuggets that we can apply in life to help us make those "good choices".

Warrior is not a mere abstract treatise on good and bad or evil and righteous. It is not just a laundry list of interesting quotes from long-dead poets, warriors, statesmen and intellects. It is living, breathing wisdom that we owe to ourselves and the next generation to embrace and pass on. Once again, Bohdi has beautifully packaged and introduced each nugget that one could almost use as a daily wisdom study guide. Buy it, read it, live it and see the improvements in your own life.

Kevin Brett

Author of: *The Way of the Martial Artist: Achieving Success in Martial Arts and in Life!*

Foreword

I was stationed in South Korea in the late 80's when I purchased Fredrick Lovret's, *The Way and the Power: Secrets of Japanese Strategy* at the Youngsan PX. At the time, I was a U.S. Army Sniper, and took my position as one of my country's "warriors" very seriously. I had always been fascinated with Asia and Asian martial arts. I had also grown up in a military family, so it was no shock that I enlisted with the U.S. Army as a senior in high school and headed off to basic training and jump school after graduating. With my interest in Asia and the martial arts, it was not surprising that I requested a transfer from the 82nd Airborne Division to South Korea after serving two years as a paratrooper. I'm still thankful for having a first sergeant that helped me obtain that transfer.

Anyhow, back to, *The Way and the Power*. Even though I served as a paratrooper and sniper during peacetime, I understood the quote of Genghis Khan's that Lovret included in his text, "There is no joy a man can feel which is greater than when he destroys his enemies and drives them before him." I understood this because it was the same feeling I felt during barroom brawls where I was able to use my high school Judo training and the subsequent Karate and Taekwondo training during my time in the Army in practical settings. I will admit that often it was my superior physical conditioning and a deep burning fire of rage that was buried deep within that awarded my victory in many of those fights, rather than any specific technique learned in a training hall. But yes, I understood the joy that Genghis Khan spoke of so many years ago.

I also understood the fundamental difference between a warrior's philosophy and that of a civilian that Lovret wrote about. I was one of those that gave up civil rights and prepared to do whatever my country asked of me, including killing and if necessary dying. I knew what I had signed up for, as I said earlier, I took my position seriously.

But that was twenty years ago. I no longer wear the uniform of the U.S. Army, and haven't for nineteen years. Getting out of the Army has been one decision I have wrestled with for years. After all, isn't the military where warriors should be? Yes and no. While I did get out of the Army, I've never left the warrior lifestyle. Throughout the years I've answered many questions with, "I'm a sniper, I can do it." One of the first times I remember answering this way was during college orientation as I entered my undergraduate studies. The advocate asked if I really wanted to take on 18 credits that included honors courses my first semester back in school. I answered with my sniper comment, which shocked her and was something she didn't understand. Most don't. I got straight "A's" that semester and the next, and continued to excel through college with my sniper/warrior training as my edge.

So yes, even though I was no longer in the military, warriorship was still very important to me. It was the warrior influence that took me back to Asia, living in both Japan and Korea, furthering my studies of Asian warrior history and martial arts. It was fascinating to see places I had studied about, and even more enlightening to train in Hapkido in the country of its origin. In fact, as I think about it, every period of my life has been defined by warriorship, and it is something that I have studied, trained for, and has been a part of me for as long as I can remember.

From the Fred Neff and Bruce Tegner books I studied as a kid in the 70's, to my Judo competitions, military years, Karate, Taekwondo, and finally settling with Hapkido as my primary martial art and how I devoured any text about warriors I could find. I used these texts to better myself and become more of the ideal I believe warriors to be. These years of training, studying, and applying principles of war to my civilian activities such as earning my business degree and subsequent law degree have given me what I like to call "The Warrior's Edge."

What I call "The Warrior's Edge" is a powerful way to live based on warriorship. Living as a warrior, even when not in the military or engaged in battle, is powerful. Face it, life can be a battle. Life can be war. The winning attitude combined with the mental and physical skills of a warrior can assist anyone in obtaining their mission in life. "The Warrior's Edge" includes having focus, discipline, and determination to take on the greatest challenges and win. However, there is so much more.

If living with "The Warrior's Edge" helps people become more focused, more determined, and more disciplined, its value would be difficult to determine, for tackling the seemingly insurmountable odds present in everyday life and conquering them is beyond measure. And while the above mentioned warrior traits are important, they are only a portion of those traits that makeup a warrior's character.

In fact, I would argue that character is the most important element of living as a warrior, more important than the physical skills, more important than weapon skills, and more important that determined discipline. The warrior's character that emphasizes honor, self-mastery, will, courage, and integrity is above all else the element that sets warriors apart from others, and allows those living by such a warrior's code to be powerful regardless of their vocation.

It's taken many years of study to realize this. When younger, I was most interested in the physical skills. I wanted to be able to place a bullet down range with precise marksmanship. I wanted to physically defeat those I faced in competition or in those ugly circumstances in barrooms and parking lots. I wanted to be able to use gun, knife, stick, or hands to defend myself. I wanted the determined discipline to win at all costs. Fortunately, through all the training, another message seeped through and permeated my consciousness and became a central focus of my warrior training. Not to the neglect of my physical training, but as an integral part of my complete warrior training. I've come to realize, as many have before me, that character training must accompany the physical training or you only create thugs, scoundrels, and unscrupulous denizens with fighting ability, not warriors.

Many martial arts have creeds or tenants that guide the character of those who train in the physical skills enabling them to hurt and possibly kill others. Martial training has been a bridge to other skills for centuries. In Musashi's *Book of Five Rings* he wrote, "With the principles of the martial arts, one makes a Way for all the arts and accomplishments, and will not misunderstand them." Reading that, I must agree with William Scott Wilson who wrote in *The Lone Samurai: The Life of Miyamoto Musashi* that the great swordsman would have surely agreed with the Chinese calligrapher who wrote, "When the Mind is correct, the brush will be also."

Studying the Kamakura period in Japan one finds there was a balance between military and cultural strengths promoted of the warrior class. I have a scroll with Musashi's "Shrike on a Withered Branch" on my office wall to remind me that Japan's sword saint was as adept with the brush as he was with the sword. We must balance the martial with the cultural in order to succeed as productive members of society. We must temper our determined disciplined drive with integrity and honor.

I've studied enough to realize there has been a romantic mysticism given to the samurai of ancient Japan and other warriors throughout history. I understand that not all samurai, and not all warriors, upheld Bushido and the moral codes associated with them. I understand that all humans falter with ethical codes. I myself have waged many ethical battles within and am ashamed to admit that I've lost many more than I prefer to say. However, I do believe that we can develop ethical reasoning skills and transform episodes of temptation into ethical right action, and I believe that is what a warrior should do. We can look past the negative aspects of history and focus on the positive lessons and traits that will enable us to live as warriors should, with honor, courage, and integrity. This study is essential for warriors, and most beneficial to everyone else.

This is where Dr. Bohdi Sanders comes in with his text *Warrior: The Way of Warriorhood*. Dr. Sanders has defined what it is to be a true warrior, and I wholeheartedly agree with his definition. It was not surprising that I recognized many of the quotes in the *Warrior Wisdom* volumes, because even though portions of our warrior lives have varied greatly, Dr. Sanders and I both share a love of studying the old warrior texts to gather wisdom from the past to apply to today's society. He took his study one step further by collecting quotes that emphasized traits such as honor, integrity, justice, respect, filial duty, physical training, mental training, and duty to one's fellow man, and organized them with thoughtful commentary on how the traits found in these older quotes are applicable today, giving the reader a guide to living as a warrior.

Dr. Sanders gives aspirants a course to follow for life, a course on living if you will, living as a warrior. This book will assist you with developing your own personal code to live by. It will inspire you to identify, codify, and follow your own warrior's code consisting of honor and integrity. It will help you live a life of character. It will help give you "The Warrior's Edge." You won't just understand what the code of the warrior is; you will live by it. If you follow the advice Dr. Sanders gives you, you will not only be a person of strong character, a modern warrior, but also someone who takes ethical action, something desperately needed in all areas of our society.

One of my favorite quotes on warriorship comes from Richard Strozzi Heckler's book *In Search of the Warrior Spirit*. Heckler wrote, "The path of the Warrior is lifelong, and mastery is often simply staying on the path." I've found this to be true, and I find the books by Dr. Sanders to be excellent guides for staying on the path.

Alain B. Burrese, J.D.

Author of: *Hard-Won Wisdom from the School of Hard Knocks*, and the DVD's *Hapkido Hoshinsul, Hapkido Cane, Streetfighting Essentials*, and the *Lock On: Joint Locking Essentials* series.

Introduction

The great Sioux chief, Sitting Bull, once stated that, "Warriors are not what you think of as warriors. The warrior is not someone who fights..." At first, this statement seems strange and contrary to what most people think, when they hear the term "warrior." How is it that the warrior is not someone who fights? Could it be that Sitting Bull didn't really know what he was talking about? Was he really "qualified" to explain what being a real warrior means? Oh, wait, wasn't he one of the warriors who defeated General Custer in the Battle of the Little Big Horn, known to the Sioux people as the Fight at Greasy Grass Creek?

Sitting Bull was one of the great warriors in one of the most well known battles fought on American soil; he must know something about warriorship. He was definitely not opposed to fighting for what he believed to be right, especially when left with no honorable alternatives. He was obviously a brave man who had the courage to meet his enemy face to face on the battlefield, as opposed to being a man who claimed that there is "never any reason for violence," or that "violence never solved anything." So what did this great warrior mean when he stated that, "Warriors are not what you think of as warriors. The warrior is not someone who fights...?"

Basically, what Sitting Bull is saying is that fighting is not the only component or even the most important part of being a warrior. He goes on to explain himself saying, "The warrior, for us, is one who sacrifices himself for the good of others. His task is to take care of the elderly, the defenseless, those who cannot provide for themselves, and above all, the children, the future of humanity." This is what he was doing at the Battle of the Little Big Horn, fighting for those who needed his protection, and this is also a very good description of the true warrior and the warrior lifestyle.

The warrior lifestyle involves much more than the ability to fight and defend yourself and those you love. It involves developing your character, living a life of honor and integrity, defending those who can't defend themselves, taking care of the elderly and your family; in short, it involves service to others along with perfecting your character. Many people seem to get hung up on the literal definition of the term "warrior." The literal definition, which can be found in most dictionaries, defines the term "warrior" as someone who is trained or experienced in warfare.

As far as the warrior lifestyle is concerned, this definition falls far short of being complete. Throughout history, when the term "warrior" has been used, it has carried with it a deeper meaning than simply "someone experienced in warfare." Warriors have been revered for their character as much as their martial arts skills. The warrior was seen as a man of character, integrity and honor, not simply someone who knew how to fight, or who was experienced in fighting. It is true that the warrior should be skilled in the art of war or in the martial arts, but this is only a small part of being a true warrior.

Gichin Funakoshi stated that the ultimate goal of karate is the perfection of human character, not the perfection of one's martial arts skills; this is basically the same thing that Sitting Bull was trying to teach us. Being a true warrior involves balance. The warrior strives for excellence in every part of his life, not only in developing his martial arts skills, but also in his everyday life. The warrior has to endeavor to perfect himself spiritually and mentally, as well as physically. While it is true that the martial arts play an important part in the life of the true warrior, the martial arts are only a part of the warrior's life.

There are many other parts of the warrior's life which must also be addressed if he is serious about living the warrior lifestyle. Character training is definitely an important part of being a warrior. Without character training, so-called "warriors" are nothing more than thugs, trained to fight, but with no knowledge of what is worth fighting for. To educate someone in the martial arts without regard to their character, is simply training a menace to society. The ancient martial arts masters knew this and refused to train those who they felt lacked the character and integrity needed to be given these dangerous skills.

Character was important to the masters of old and was taken into account before someone was trained. Today, the martial arts have become big business and anyone with enough money can obtain as much training as they want, no matter how poor their character may be. Are these people warriors simply because they have purchased years of training and know how to fight? Are gang members who know how to fight warriors? Well, if you go by the literal definition, your answer would have to be yes, but if you go by the definition that I use for the true warrior, the answer is definitely no.

My definition of a true warrior is someone who has the ability and will to fight to protect himself, his friends, his family, and his ideals, and at the same time, seeks the perfection of his own character through a life lived with honor, integrity, and an unflinching dedication to what is right according to his own code of ethics. The ability to fight is only a small part of this definition. The true warrior has to develop more than his martial arts skills. The qualities of the true warrior go much deeper than that.

Warriors should exhibit the best qualities among men. The true warrior makes a firm decision to try to perfect his character and to live by a strict code of ethics. His word is his honor. His duty stays fresh on his mind. He lives life a little more seriously than most, but at the same time lives life to its fullest. He sees through the veil of appearances covering most parts of this world, but does so without looking down on those who are less perceptive.

Family and friends are important to him, and they know that they can always count on him for protection and help in their times of need. He bases his decisions on his code of ethics, and he instinctively knows right from wrong, and chooses right. He knows that at times there is a difference between what is right and what is legal, and what is wrong and what is illegal. As Lao Tzu taught, "Highly evolved people have their own conscience as pure law."

The true warrior is able to hold his head high with honor because he knows that he lives his life to the best of his ability, with honor and integrity. His code is ingrained in his spirit and is a part of his being. Warriors walk alone much of the time, as they prefer solitude to the company of lesser men. The warrior is a man who shoots for excellence in everything he does. These are the things which make someone a true warrior and the development of these traits leads to the warrior lifestyle.

Warrior: The Way of Warriorhood is a journey through the wisdom and character of the warrior lifestyle. Bushido literally means, "the way of the warrior," and that is what *Warrior: The Way of Warriorhood* is all about – the way of the warrior. This book looks at the many aspects of the life of the warrior, from character training to physical training, and everything in between, and hopefully will serve as an interesting guide for you on your journey towards your ultimate goal.

Bohdi Sanders, PhD

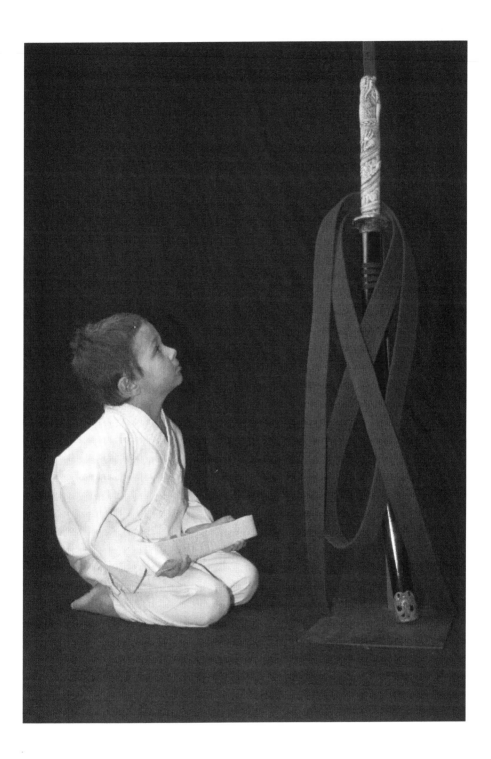

Warrior

The Way of Warriorhood

1

To protect the weak and defenseless
The Chivalric Code of Charlemagne

To those who have been given much, much is required. Warriors have been given specific training in martial arts and in the knowledge of self-defense. Hopefully they have also been instructed in ways to, not only defend themselves, but also to use their acquired skills to defend others. Warriors have a duty to defend others when it is in their power to do so.

There are a lot of people who do not have the same training or skills that the warrior has developed over his years of training. They are not able to protect themselves, much less those around them. These people live their lives depending on the goodwill of others. For various reasons, they have never developed the ability to fend off an attacker. Most have grown up in a fairly sheltered environment and really do not understand the psychology of the predator. The warrior is their only defense.

The warrior, on the other hand, has studied the art of self-defense. He knows the mind of the predator and what the criminal looks for in a victim. The skills that he has trained so hard to perfect are designed to keep him and his friends and family safe from those who would prey on the innocent. They have been given much knowledge; therefore they have a duty to use this knowledge to help the weak and the defenseless. Wherever you are, those around you should be a little safer because you are there.

2

The more you sweat in training, the less you bleed in battle.
Navy Seal Maxim

Staying in top physical shape is important to the warrior. Many times physical encounters can end up being won by the man who is in the best shape. If the fight ends up going for more than just a few seconds, you had better have a good aerobic capacity. It won't matter how skilled your techniques are or how powerful your punches are, if you are so out of breath that you can't stand up straight after a 60 second encounter.

Physical fitness is even more important if the fight ends up going to the ground and becoming a grappling contest. This doesn't even take into account the fact that you may have to face multiple attackers. Even professional boxers can become winded after a hard three minute round of one on one boxing, and these guys train hard and long. It is imperative that you not only train for good form and useful techniques, but that you also train for endurance. Endurance training will help ensure that you have enough staying power to not lose a contest because of poor aerobic capacity.

You should be cross training. Don't just focus on one area of training. Think balance. Think of your overall goals. What is the overall purpose of your training? What do you want to get out of your training routine? Remember, no matter what you are doing, it is important for you to know why you are doing it. For the warrior, the answer is that you are training hard, so you will bleed less.

3

The greatest enemies, and the ones we must mainly combat, are within.

Cervantes

Everyone has enemies, even the most jovial, well-liked person has people who would love to see him crash and burn. You have enemies, even if you don't realize it, but most of your enemies are no threat. Most of them don't care enough or are not malevolent enough to truly cause you any problems. In fact, you may never have to deal with your enemies at all, at least not your external enemies, but there are enemies which we all have to deal with on a regular basis, and as Cervantes stated, they come from within.

These enemies are the ones that the warrior must conquer in his quest to live the warrior lifestyle. Just like external enemies, these internal enemies are different for each person. Some may take the form of laziness or fear, while others may take the form of anger and temper. Everyone has their own individual enemies to deal with during their journey on the path of the warrior. The important thing is that you do not let your enemies defeat you and prevent you from obtaining your goals.

You know what your own personal enemy is and it is your responsibility to figure out how to defeat this enemy. There are no small, insignificant enemies. Each one has the capacity to do some damage and set you back in your quest. Don't let your internal enemies slide – crush them and render them powerless. This is an important part of being a true warrior.

4

Make your enemy think that your normal force is extraordinary, and your extraordinary is your normal.

Sun Tzu

Sun Tzu wrote the above quote in his timeless classic, *The Art of War*. This is a great quote to meditate on and let the implications sink into your spirit. Part of warfare, whether you are talking about military tactics or the art of self-defense, is attacking the mind of your enemy, and this is exactly what Sun Tzu is telling you to do here. This is psychological warfare at its best. If your opponent thinks that your normal force is extraordinary, he wonders, in the back of his mind, just how devastating you will be if you kick it up a notch.

This not only causes him to fear your abilities, but it also causes him to doubt his ability to actually defeat you. Once he starts to doubt himself or his skills, your enemy is on his way to being defeated. Thomas Cleary translated several ancient samurai writings in his book, *Training the Samurai Mind*, and he tells us that the key to the warrior's heart is maintaining courage.

It is extremely hard for your enemy to maintain his courage when he truly believes that he cannot defeat you. Use psychological warfare to your advantage. Seed your enemy's mind with doubt and fear. Cause him to doubt his own skills, while at the same time seeing you as a stalwart of steel. Make him think that your normal force is extraordinary, and that your best is simply undefeatable. Allow his own doubt to defeat him.

5

How we train is how we shall respond.
Kelly S. Worden

Warriors of the past took their training much more seriously than people seem to today. Musashi stated that one should train more than he sleeps. Now, in today's society, we realize that this is impossible, unless you are independently wealthy. We all have to make a living and provide for our families. There are just too many responsibilities on our plates today to devote six to eight hours each day to our training. Because of the time constraints on our lives, it is even more important to be focused during our training time.

The time that we have to train is much too short and it is vital that we be focused and mindful during our training. How you perform during your practice time is ultimately how you will perform in a time of crisis. Your training matters. Practice does not make perfect; perfect practice makes perfect. You should take your training seriously. Don't just haphazardly walk through your training sessions like a zombie. Make them count. Push yourself and strive for improvement each time you enter the dojo.

Master Funakoshi taught that you should always take your training deadly serious. The reason for this is pretty obvious, especially considering the type of skills that warriors are training to obtain. When the time comes that you need to call on the skills that you are trying to perfect, it could very well be a deadly serious situation. At that point in time you will be glad that you took your training seriously and applied yourself to your training, spirit, mind and body.

6

Someone out there is training.
Law Enforcement Maxim

There are many days when you will not feel like training. The opportunities to do something else in place of your training are endless. It's all too easy to think to yourself, "I just don't feel like it today," or "It won't hurt to take today off." The problem is that one day turns into one week, and one week turns into one month, and one month turns into two, etc. We are creatures of habit. Once you start getting into the habit of not training, it is easy to continue on that path.

You have to find ways to continue to keep yourself motivated. One way to stay motivated is to contemplate the fact that somewhere out there, somebody else is training, and training hard and seriously. This guy is not taking the day, week, month, or summer off. He is honing his martial arts skills to perfection. He is pumping weights and his strength and muscle mass are increasing weekly. He's not training his character though, but that's okay; he doesn't need character to achieve his goals. You see, he is not training to be a warrior; he is training to perfect his skills as a predator.

If he continues to train hard, while at the same time you continue to take time off and take your training a bit less serious, the gap between his skills and your skills will widen. This is a dangerous situation for the warrior to be in because in the event that your paths cross, and your duty requires you to confront this guy, you will lose. Someone out there is training, are you?

7

The soul is dyed the color of its thoughts.
Heraclitus

Many people believe that their thoughts don't really matter. They think that their thoughts don't matter as long as they don't act on their negative thoughts. What they fail to realize though is that everyone's thoughts contain certain energy patterns. Physicists are now proving that your thoughts actually do have power; they are not just harmless little things that don't matter.

Heraclitus knew this many centuries ago. He tells us that your thoughts have an effect on your soul. He goes on to say, "The content of your character is your choice. Day by day, what you choose, what you think and what you do is who you become. Your integrity is your destiny... it is the light that guides your way." Your thoughts are much more important to your character development than you may suspect.

Thought precedes action. Many scientists today believe that if you continue to think about something, what you think about will eventually find a way to manifest itself in your life. If this is true, it means that what you think about is extremely important. It has already been proven that your thoughts control your emotions; thus to control your emotions, which every warrior must do, you must control your thoughts.

Controlling your thoughts is the ultimate test of your self-discipline. Once you get to the point where you can control your thoughts, you will be well on your way to mastering the warrior lifestyle. Control your thoughts and you control your destiny.

8

Power of the mind in infinite while brawn is limited.

Koichi Tohei

Even the biggest, most ripped bodybuilders have their limits as to how much muscle mass they can add to their body. No matter how much you work out or train, there is only so much you can do to perfect yourself physically. This is just the way it is. Although "no limits" is a popular slogan at many gyms, everyone's body has certain limits. The mind, on the other hand, has no limits.

The power of the mind is far beyond anything that anyone has yet to experience. It is said that even the most brilliant men only use approximately 10% of their mind. These are the most intelligent individuals on the planet, and they only use 10% of their minds! This obviously leaves ample room for the development of the mind. When you look at intelligence in this manner, it is plain to see that the power of the human mind is truly infinite.

This is important to the warrior. The warrior has to train his mind, as well as his body. Mental training is just as important as physical training. The best martial arts skills in the world will do you no good if your mind panics during a crucial encounter. Your mind should be the first weapon used in any encounter, and the sharpest weapon in your arsenal. Don't get so caught up in your physical training that you neglect your mental training. Everything that you do has a mental component to it. Neglecting to train your mind, as well as your body, is unbalanced training. Think balance. Train your mind as well as your body.

9

One must transcend techniques so that the art becomes an artless art, growing out of the unconscious.
Daisetsu Suzuki

Today it seems that many so-called martial artists get "bored" with their training because they find that they have to do the same kicks, punches, katas, etc. over and over again. The attention span of people today is much shorter than in times past. Our lifestyle today has changed to the point that our news comes in short 10-20 second spurts. Even our educational systems have changed to accommodate the short attention span of today's students.

This is not how the warrior should train. It takes thousands of repetitions to perfect your techniques. You must pay attention to every detail of your kicks, punches, throws, stances, and movements. In order to internalize the elements of each technique, you must practice them over and over. There are no short cuts. You must perform them time and time again for them to become a part of you. When your back is against the wall, your techniques must be part of your unconsciousness in order for them to be effective.

You will not have time to stop and think about what to do or how to do it; it has to come naturally and automatically. When you get to this point, you will find that your techniques flow without any conscious thought on your part. Your mind will transcend your technique. You will be in mushin. Mushin is a mental state where your body goes on auto-pilot. You simply respond as you should. This state can only come from practice and experience. Transcend the mind and enter mushin.

10

A warrior's heart is like a sword; it must be cleaned daily.
Billy Shearer

Perfecting your character takes a lot of effort. It is not a goal that you accomplish and then you can relax because you have "made it." Developing your character is an ongoing process which never ends. There will always be something or someone who will try to throw a monkey wrench into your peaceful existence. Controlling your thoughts and your emotions takes work, but the more that you practice these skills, the easier they will become.

The art of self-control is like every other endeavor; you will have good days and bad days in your quest to perfect this skill. Nobody is perfect, especially when it comes to controlling thoughts and emotions. There will be days when you fall short of your goal. I can assure you that you will have days in which you allow your anger or impatience to get the best of you, just as you will have days when your back kick does not click for whatever reason, but it is important that you don't quit.

When you find that you are having a bad day with your physical training, you don't say this is not working and never go back to the dojo. The same goes for your mental training. When you have a bad day, go home and relax, meditate, and cleanse your heart and mind. Get things back in balance and know that every day you start with a clean slate. Once you actually get your heart clean, it is much easier to keep it clean. If you find the same things continue to throw you off balance time after time, go to the source and remove the root of your of your problem. Think about this.

11

Abandoning the ego
is the secret of right living.
Taisen Deshimaru

The warrior can't afford to allow his ego to get in the way of his goals and his responsibilities. There are a lot of people in the martial arts who are driven solely by their egos. These people are not true warriors. The warrior never fights for issues which are based on ego. Ego is one's exaggerated sense of his own self-importance. It is a feeling of superiority when compared to other people. Ego has nothing to do with honor; the ego has to do with pride.

Warriors should not allow feelings of self-importance, superiority, or pride to control their emotions. It is your duty, as a warrior, to help the weak and the needy, not to look down on them and to feel that you are above them. Abandon feelings of self-importance and concentrate on your character and your duty as a warrior. No one respects an egotistical person, no matter how much character or integrity he has. Nobody likes to feel inferior. This is important to remember.

True, the warrior should be superior to others in many ways: character, integrity, honor, skills, etc., but you must control the feeling that you actually *are* superior. Don't think about how you compare to others as far as these traits go. Simply do the best that you can do to perfect your own character and to live right, and leave others to be responsible for their own character. Abandon your ego and develop your character.

12

One who is good at battle does not get angry.
Lao Tzu

You don't have to get angry in order to get your adrenaline pumping in a confrontation. In fact, if you find yourself in a physical confrontation, getting angry will actually hinder your performance. Anger causes your mind to become confused and to think less clearly. It causes your actions to be controlled by your emotions rather than your rational mind. Letting your emotions control your actions is always a dangerous proposition.

Instead of getting angry in these situations, you should go into mushin. Mushin literally means "mind, no mind." This simply means that you are acting without consciously thinking about what you are doing. You are allowing your subconscious mind to take control, not your anger. This is why you perform the same techniques and the same fight scenarios over and over again in the dojo. This secures the techniques into your subconscious mind so that you can perform them without thinking, when you need them.

Mushin is much like driving a car. When you first started driving, you had to concentrate on every part of the driving process. You had to consciously think to yourself to turn on the turn signal and to start slowing down, but after several years of driving, simple things like turning your turn signal on, or slowing down when you come to a turn, come naturally. You don't have to consciously think to yourself, "Now I need to start slowing down." You just do it naturally, without thinking about it. This is the mind in mushin. You can perform actions without your mind actually telling you what to do because you have performed them so many times that they are now automatic.

13

**I come to you with only empty hands.
I have no weapons, but should I be forced
to defend myself, my principles or my honor,
should it be a matter of life and death, or right or
wrong; then here are my weapons, my empty hands.**
Ed Parker

In today's society, most people do not walk around carrying weapons, at least most well intentioned people don't, unless they have a concealed weapons permit. Most likely, you don't carry a weapon when you are out on the town. Therefore, your weapons have to be your hands and your feet. This is why you train in the martial arts. True, you probably have some weapons training thrown into the mix, but you don't walk around carrying a bow staff or any of the other various weapons which are taught in most dojos.

Notice that I said that most well intentioned people don't carry weapons. You can pretty much count on the people with less than honorable intentions to be carrying some sort of weapon. Never expect a fair fight when you are forced to defend yourself, your family or your friends. Predators and thugs do not fight fair. They have no sense of honor.

They have goals, and their objective is to fulfill their goals by any means necessary. The point to all of this is you had better be prepared. Keep your weapons sharp and ready to be used at a moment's notice. Your weapons are useless if you are not proficient in the use of those weapons. Train hard and be prepared to use your weapons to defend yourself if circumstances require you to do so. Your empty hands are your weapons.

14

Try not! Do, or do not. There is no try.
Yoda

Okay, you may think it is kind of strange that I would include a quote from a fictional character in the *Warrior Wisdom Series*, but this quote actually contains a lot of wisdom for the warrior. When someone asks you if you are going to do something and you respond with, "I'll try" that is nothing more a than flimsy way to put the other person off. The warrior is not afraid of commitment. He knows whether or not he is willing to complete a task or not. Don't say you will try. Either say that you will do it or say that you won't do it.

As our little green friend stated, there is no try, you either do it or you don't do it. Don't be afraid to make firm decisions. If someone asks you to do something, and you know that you are not planning on doing it, don't say "I'll try" in an attempt to put them off. Be honest enough to say, "I would like to, but I just don't have the time now, so I can't commit to it." You will find that most people appreciate your honesty.

Saying, "I'll try to do it," is just a way to avoid commitment. This should especially be avoided on the path of the warrior. You don't try to live a life of honor and integrity; you live a life of honor and integrity. You don't try to make time for your training; you make time for your training. You don't try to be prepared to defend your family and friends; you do defend your family and friends. You don't try to live the lifestyle of the warrior; you live the lifestyle of the warrior. Make a decision and then follow through with it. Try not! Do, or do not.

15

The warrior is not led by others; but by remaining true to his convictions.
F. J. Chu

As a warrior, it is up to you to decide what you stand for and what your standards will be. You cannot be led or misled by the winds of public opinion. Don't be like some politician who doesn't really have any true convictions, but rather waits until he sees how the public feels, and then sides with the majority. Throughout history, the sages have told us that the majority of people are not people of integrity and honor; you should never be influenced by people who do not live their life with honor.

Be independent of the opinions of others. Don't be easily influenced by what they say or what they believe. You have to take the time to meditate on what you know is right and wrong. Know what your code of ethics is and do not allow the arguments of others to cause you to doubt what you know is right. You must remain true to your convictions, even if everyone else disagrees with you.

This is part of the warrior lifestyle. You have to know what you believe and why you believe it. You have to know why you are living this lifestyle and what sets you, as a warrior, apart from everyone else. Your convictions are a major part of what makes you different. If you allow others to sway your convictions, what makes you any different than them? It takes courage to live up to your convictions and courage is one of the character traits which sets the warrior apart from lesser men. Have courage and stay true to your convictions.

16

Style doesn't matter,
what works is what's important.
Mitsusuke Harada

When it comes to defending yourself on the street, style doesn't matter. You use anything and everything that you can in order to assure, first that you are safe, then that the threat is completely neutralized. There is no such thing as "fair" or "unfair" when you find yourself in a life-or-death situation. This is a hard concept for some people to grasp.

You hear some guys saying things such as, "I would never throw sand in someone's eyes during a fight, that's not fair." or "That guy hit Jack with a brick, that's fighting dirty!" Actually, fighting dirty only applies to sporting events, not to actual self-defense. If someone is about to attack you with the intent of doing some major damage to your person, and there is a brick lying by your foot, you are being foolish not to pick up the brick and use it. I can't emphasize this enough. In an actual fight, you use everything available to ensure your safety and the safety of those around you!

This has nothing to do with being dishonorable or taking cheap shots. Considering that the warrior will not engage in a fight unless all other options have failed, the fight must be a necessity. You have already acted honorably by trying everything in your power to avoid a physical confrontation. Once this point is reached, the only "rules" are to protect yourself and to destroy your enemy – by any means necessary.

17

To lead untrained people to war is to throw them away.
Confucius

At first this quote by Confucius may seem obvious. Of course no one would send untrained people to war. They wouldn't stand a chance, especially if they were going into battle against well trained enemies. No one would do this, right? Well, let's back up and take a closer look at this. Actually, this is happening all the time in the United States. Does this shock you? Let me clarify this statement for you.

There are dojos all across our country that are taking money from people and claiming to train them to defend themselves. They sign them up for a long-term contract. They train them and hand out black belts almost as easily as elementary teachers hand out gold stars to their students. Once these unsuspecting martial arts students reach the level of black belt or even start to get anywhere close to it, they start to believe that they are prepared to defend themselves.

It doesn't matter that this person has never been in any kind of realistic fighting situation. They believe that they are a human weapon; after all, a black belt is supposed to be a martial arts expert. These people leave the dojo with a false sense of their expertise and an over inflated ego to go along with it. Does the instructor know that his students may not be able to defend themselves? He should. Does he explain to them that there is a huge difference between sparring in a dojo and defending himself against a seasoned street thug? If he doesn't, he is sending the lambs to slaughter.

18

I have seen the best karate. All that really matters is what kind of human being you are.
Masami Tsuruoka

This quote is very interesting. At first you may think, "This guy is probably someone who couldn't hack the martial arts training, so he has decided that all that really matters is what kind of human being you are." But this is not the case. Masami Tsuruoka is actually a martial arts master. He has taught hundreds of students and has dedicated his life to the martial arts.

Masami Tsuruoka is not alone in his philosophy of the martial arts. Many of the older martial arts masters have made similar statements. He is not saying that it is not important to train in martial arts, but rather that character training is the most important part of your training, especially if you are interested in living the warrior lifestyle. What matters in everyday life is what kind of human being you are.

You will have many, many more opportunities, outside the dojo, to use your character training than you will to use your martial arts. In fact, you will find that you use your character training on a daily basis. Think about how many decisions you make each day. What determines which choices you make? If you are on the path of the warrior, the answer is your honor, character and integrity. What kind of human being are you? What kind of human being will you be tomorrow? This is really what the warrior lifestyle is all about – perfecting your character and becoming the person that you should be.

19

One should always be willing to assist others selflessly and unconditionally by offering one's skills and achievements to serve them.
Lao Tzu

Lao Tzu, the author of the *Tao Te Ching*, is speaking to everyone when he wrote that one should always be willing to help others, but not everyone adheres to his instruction. Most people want to know what is in it for them or what could happen if they actually get involved. They prefer to use their skills and achievements to serve themselves.

The warrior, on the other hand, knows that he has a sacred duty to follow this teaching from the *Tao Te Ching*. He knows that it is part of who he is to serve and protect. Selflessly, the warrior offers his martial arts knowledge and skills to protect those who are helpless or weak. He is willing to put his life on the line to protect those around him if the situation demands that he do so. The skills that he has worked so hard to obtain are used to keep his friends and family safe.

It doesn't matter that many times his efforts and intentions go unnoticed and unappreciated; he continues with his duty despite what others say or do. He realizes that he is not assisting others for any type of reward or celebrity. He is serving others selflessly and unconditionally because that is the kind of person he has decided to be. Living by his own standards, and doing what is right is all that concerns him. And he knows that what is right is using his skills, wisdom and knowledge to serve others and make their lives better if he can.

20

The path of the warrior is lifelong, and mastery is often simply staying on the path.
Richard Strozzi Heckler

The warrior lifestyle is a journey, not a destination. It is a lifelong approach to living your life, day by day, by the standards and code of ethics that you have set for yourself. To stay on this path you have to follow certain directions, just as you would follow a road map or signs to make sure that you remain on the right highway. You can't just aimlessly go through life with no direction.

Character training is the road map to the path of the warrior. You must study the qualities that make up the character of the warrior. Meditate on these character traits until they become a part of your spirit; until they become who you truly are deep inside. No one is born with all of the character traits which make the warrior an extraordinary man. These traits have to be developed through study, training, meditation, and learning from your mistakes.

Yes, the warrior makes mistakes. No one is perfect. The difference in the ordinary man and the warrior is when the warrior makes a mistake he learns from his error and makes the necessary changes that will help him make better decisions next time. He is constantly trying to improve his character. His mistakes do not mean defeat unless he allows them to cause him to give up the path of the warrior. Mastery will come if you simply stay on the path and continue to learn and improve your character every day. Don't get frustrated with the apparent lack of progress in your journey. Remember, this is a journey, not a destination.

21

Hide your purpose.
Baltasar Gracian

Baltasar Gracian is one of my favorite authors. His writing contains an abundance of worldly wisdom. Here he tells you to "hide your purpose." Don't confuse this with being dishonest. He is not talking about lying here, but rather he is writing about not disclosing too much information. It is much easier for your enemies to prepare to disrupt your plans, your tactics, and your strategies if you make clear to them what you are thinking.

Many people constantly talk and disclose personal information which they should keep private. Your speech can cause many problems for you, especially when you are not careful concerning what you are saying and who you are speaking to. Your enemies will always welcome conversation with you if they know that you are careless with your speech. Disclosing personal information is rarely to your advantage.

It is much wiser to keep your personal information to yourself. Don't reveal your purpose to just anyone. You never know who they will talk to later, your friend has a friend, and your friend's friend has a friend. Think before you speak. Think about why you feel the need to discuss your plans or your strategies with someone else. If it is to obtain wisdom from a wise friend, that is one thing; if it is because you feel the need to make conversation, that is another thing altogether. Be careful about who you share your purpose with, and always think about all the possible consequences.

22

Never imagine that you are safe after you deal a blow to your opponent.
Yagyu Tajimanokami Munenori

The warrior knows that fighting is a serious business and should never be entered into lightly. You should always do everything in your power to avoid a physical encounter. It is much better to avoid danger or to defeat your enemy without actually having to result to violence if at all possible. Never use your martial arts expertise unless you have no other recourse.

This said, when you do have to resort to violence to defend yourself or someone else, don't play around. Don't assume that if you punch a threatening street thug in the nose, he has learned his lesson and will then straighten up, shake hands, and change his attitude. In the movie *The Karate Kid*, Daniel, the character played by Ralph Machio, has an encounter on the beach at the beginning of the movie with another kid. This kid punched Daniel in the stomach, then Daniel punched him in the face and said, "Okay, now we are even," as he offered to shake his hand. The other kid proceeded to thoroughly thrash Daniel.

The point here is that if the situation is important enough to resort to using your martial arts skills, it is serious enough to do some major damage before you consider the matter settled. If it is not serious enough to dish out a hard core pounding, then you are in the wrong if you decide to use your martial arts training in this instance. Insight and discernment have to be your guide

23

The results are only shadows and echoes of our actions.
Counsels of the Great Yu

Every action has its own consequence. Whether you call it the law of cause and effect or whether you call it karma, the end result is the same; everything that you do, say or think has a consequence connected with it. There is literally nothing that you can do, say or think which doesn't have some kind of effect on your life. At this point I imagine that you may be thinking to yourself something such as, "Well, if I am sitting on my patio and I say something completely meaningless, it has no affect on anything at all."

Let's examine that statement. It actually does have an effect; it can affect your emotions and/or your thought processes. Now, granted the effect may be minimal, but nevertheless, there will be a consequence of some kind. The same thing goes for your thoughts. You may believe that your thoughts actually don't have consequences, but on the contrary, every thought contains a certain energy, which at the very least has an effect on your emotions. Science has proven that your thoughts can in fact change your body chemistry, so in actuality, we don't fully realize all of the consequences that our thoughts may have.

This is true for all of your actions. There is no way to actually know for sure what the consequences of our actions really are. Some may be obvious, but others may be so far removed from the initial action that it is impossible to connect the result to the origin. What the warrior needs to stay focused on is that all of his actions are important. Everything matters on the path of warriorship.

24

Courtesy should be apparent in all our actions and words and in all aspects of daily life.
Masutatsu Oyama

Courtesy is a character trait which all warriors should practice. Too many "warriors" seem to only be concerned with manners and courtesy when they are in the dojo or around what they consider to be important people. Courtesy should not be a characteristic that we display only on special occasions. It should be a normal part of the warrior's daily life.

Masutatsu Oyama tells us that it should permeate all aspects of our daily life, from our actions to our words. Courtesy should be so much a part of your life that if someone were asked to describe you, one of the first things that they would say would be that you are extremely courteous and kind. Winston Churchill went as far as to say, "When you have to kill a man, it costs nothing to be polite."

Be courteous and polite to everyone regardless of how they act. These traits should be common practice for the warrior. Of course, there will be times when you may have to temporarily bend this rule to get your point across, but this should definitely be the exception to the rule for someone on the warrior path. Be nice. Be nice until it is time to not be nice. The thing that the warrior has to realize is that even when it is time to "not to be nice," he must still maintain his own standards. Think about what Winston Churchill said, "It costs nothing to be polite." Using manners is part of who you are, and you don't change who you are because of the circumstances.

25

When the enemy presents an opportunity, speedily take advantage of it.
Sun Tzu

Everyone makes mistakes. It doesn't matter who you are or what you are doing, you will make a mistake at some point. This is a key point to remember when it comes to any physical encounter. At some point in any encounter, your attacker will make a mistake. You just have to be patient and ready to take advantage of the mistake when it happens.

Don't panic and rush into action. Be patient. Remember, the first rule of self-defense is to make sure that you are safe, not to beat your opponent. Keep yourself safe until the opening presents itself, and then you launch your attack. Don't delay. The window of opportunity will only be open for a split second. If you delay you will miss your chance, and there may not be another opening.

Speed is of utmost importance. If you don't act fast when you get an opening, you allow your attacker to recover from his mistake and regroup. Don't let him off the hook. When he screws up, make it a costly mistake. Sun Tzu also tells us that opportunities multiply as they are seized. Basically, once the attacker starts to make mistakes, if you take advantage of his mistakes, he will start to fall apart. When this happens, destroy him as he continues to slip up. This is the art of self-defense. There is no such thing as "fighting dirty" when you are in a real fight. Think about this.

26

Man is only as strong as his convictions and beliefs.
Kensho Furuya

Your convictions and beliefs are a major part of who you are as a warrior. They determine your commitment to the warrior lifestyle, to your training, to your friends and family, and to your overall self-improvement. Without strong convictions concerning right and wrong, a warrior has no compass for his life. His convictions are the driving force behind his code of ethics.

Without a strong belief in the importance of honor and integrity, you will find that these traits become less important to you, and consequently, they will become flexible. Situational ethics is not fitting for the warrior. Honor and integrity should never be compromised. It takes a lot of courage to maintain your honor and integrity in the face of those who neither understand nor respect these qualities, and who will verbally attack you concerning your beliefs.

Without courage, you will stumble, and courage requires strong convictions. The warrior lifestyle is not the easiest path to take. You have to believe in the value of living your life according to the strict standards that are required for this lifestyle. You will not be successful if you don't know *why* you have chosen the path of the warrior. You have to have a strong belief in what you are doing and know *why* you are doing it. Without conviction, you have a major chink in your armor.

27

Calamity springs from carelessness.
Gichin Funakoshi

Everything matters. You will see me make this statement often as you read through the *Warrior Wisdom Series*. Don't take the small things for granted. Carelessness in taking care of the small things, the things that you think are not really important and don't really matter, can cost you big time. It is important that you take your time and pay attention to details. This applies to everything in your life, and that includes your martial arts.

Don't be careless concerning the fundamentals of your martial arts techniques. Too many people are only interested in advancing as fast as possible through their system to get to that prized black belt. In the process, they don't really take the time to learn the fundamentals as well as they should. They don't really understand the underlying principles behind the techniques. This is equivalent to building a house on a poor foundation. There will come a time when this poor foundation will cause some major problems.

As Master Funakoshi pointed out, calamity springs from carelessness. If you have a shaky foundation in your martial arts training, there may come a time when that could cause you some major problems. You can't afford to have your self-defense techniques built on a poor foundation. Don't be careless in anything, especially your martial arts training. Don't be in such a hurry. Shoot for excellence. It is quality, not appearance that matters.

28

Every single word is of great importance to a samurai.
The Hagakura

The warrior should be careful with his words. His word is his honor. When you tell someone that you will do something, you have just given your word. As a warrior, you have entered into a verbal contract with this person. It would be dishonorable to break this contract by not following through on what you said you would do. You owe this person. They are counting on you, as a man of your word, to do what you say you will.

Another reason that you should be careful with your speech is that everything you say can and will be held against you, if at all possible, by your enemies. Your enemies are looking for ways to trip you up. They are looking for a weakness in your life, a place where they feel they can attack you. Many times we provide our enemies with the means to our own destruction through our own speech. Careless words can come back to hurt you in ways that you could never imagine.

The ancient sages knew the importance of being careful with your speech, even in ancient times when there was no internet, television, or press listening to their every word. They knew that your words could cause you much grief. Over and over the great sages warn of the importance of controlling your speech. If it was that important in ancient times, how much more important is it to watch what you say in today's society?

29

To be prepared is half the victory.
Cervantes

No matter what you are doing, being prepared for the task is a must. Whether you are going hiking in the mountains or taking your wife or girlfriend out to dinner, you need to be prepared for the worst possible scenario. Just as you don't want to be caught in the mountains in some unexpected, emergency situation without the proper gear and supplies, you also don't want to be unprepared for the unexpected surprises when you are on the streets. Being caught off guard and unprepared in either case can be very dangerous.

It is easy to be prepared for a trip to the mountains. You educate yourself about the dangers that, though unlikely, you could possibly face, and you prepare for every possible scenario as best as you can. You pack matches, emergency gear, your hiking stick, a knife, etc. You are careful not to neglect taking the proper precautions when you are set to spend a day or longer in the mountains and you should do the same when you leave your home to go into the city.

Educate yourself on the possible dangers that you may encounter, although you know that these dangers are fairly rare. Know how to deal with these "emergency situations" should you find yourself caught up in one of these scenarios. Be prepared and aware. Don't wander mindlessly around town, anymore than you would mindlessly hike through the mountains. Sure, running into a street thug set on doing you bodily harm when you are going out to dinner is rare, but mountain lion attacks are also fairly rare, yet every year we read about people being killed in both situations.

30

One should be careful to improve himself continually.
Shu Ching

This goes to the root of the warrior lifestyle. The warrior must be constantly improving himself in every area of his life. In Japanese this concept is called "kaizen," which literally means constant, never-ending improvement. Constant, never-ending improvement is exactly what the warrior lifestyle is all about. Warriors must strive to improve themselves spiritually, mentally, and physically.

Many of the warriors from throughout history attempted to do just this in their lives. They took their spiritual beliefs seriously and spent time daily reflecting and meditating on those beliefs. They knew what they believed and why they believed it. Warriors made attempts to improve their minds through studying and learning during times of peace. Keeping their bodies fit and prepared for battle was a top priority, as was keeping their marital arts skills ready for when they might be called on to use them.

The same should apply to modern day warriors. Strive to be well rounded. Know what you believe in spiritually and make time for that part of your life. Do all that you can to educate yourself. Read and learn about a variety of subjects. Study books on wisdom and apply it to your life. Keep yourself in shape and make sure that you continually add to your martial arts skills and that they are sharp and ready to be used when needed. This is the warrior lifestyle. It is a lifestyle of excellence, not complacency.

31

Tomorrow belongs to those who prepare today.
African Proverb

I have already touched on being prepared for whatever you may encounter, whether you are going out for a day of recreation or going out on the town. Being prepared is extremely important and the only safe course of action for the warrior to take. You can prepare for some things at the spur of the moment. For example, if you start to walk out the door and it looks as though it may rain, you can turn back and get your umbrella just in case. Other situations take a bit more preparation in order to be prepared.

Self-defense is one of the things that you need to prepare for well in advance. You can't decide to go out to a late show, and just before you walk out the door, decide that you need to learn a few self-defense techniques just in case you run into trouble. This is ridiculous. As you know, it takes months or years of constant training to be competent to defend yourself. It is not something that you can put off until you happen to think about the possibility of needing it one night.

Your preparation in the area of self-defense has to be an ongoing process. If you want to be prepared for tomorrow's surprise encounter, you have to prepare for it today. This is what being prepared actually means. You are preparing now for what may happen sometime down the line. If you find yourself in a situation where you need your skills, they will be ready. If you find that you don't need them, they are still available to you. Either way, you are prepared.

32

Don't hit at all if it can be avoided, but never hit softly.
Theodore Roosevelt

It is a principle of karate that you never attack first. The meaning behind this saying is that the warrior should not use his martial arts skills in a threatening or bullying manner. It goes without saying, that doing so is a dishonorable act and is not fitting for anyone who is traveling the path of the warrior. You should only use your martial arts skills in cases of self-defense or the defense of others, and then, only if you have no other recourse.

If at all possible, avoid a physical confrontation. Try to calm the other person down if he is in an excited mental state. Use your mind and mediation skills to resolve the problem. This is much harder to do than it sounds, and these types of skills should be a part of your training as a warrior. If your conversational skills fail, try and walk away if it is an option.

It is when your efforts to compromise or to resolve the issue peacefully have failed, that you may have to resort to using your martial arts skills. Although you should avoid this position if you can, once things evolve to this point, it is game on. Never strike softly as a warning. This person's chances to resolve things peacefully have been exhausted. When the situation degrades to a physical issue, strike hard, strike fast, and strike until there is no doubt left about the possibility of clear and present danger. Do what you can to avoid a fight, but once engaged, be deadly serious about coming out the victor. As Shaka Zulu said, "Never leave an enemy standing."

33

Warriors are not what you think of as warriors. The warrior is not someone who fights.
Sitting Bull

You may think that this is a very strange statement coming from a famous warrior, a warrior who fought in one of the most famous battles in our country's history, the Battle of Little Big Horn. What does Sitting Bull mean by his statement that the warrior is not someone who fights? It goes without saying that the warrior is someone who certainly has the ability to fight when the occasion calls for it. So what was this warrior trying to say to us?

Basically, what Sitting Bull is saying is that fighting is not the only component or the most important part of being a warrior. He goes on to explain himself, "The warrior, for us, is one who sacrifices himself for the good of others. His task is to take care of the elderly, the defenseless, those who cannot provide for themselves, and above all, the children, the future of humanity."

This is a very good description of the warrior lifestyle. You will find these same characteristics of a warrior throughout history. Of course you find a different definition of what a warrior is in the dictionary, but true warriorship goes much deeper than defining it as only someone experienced in warfare. It involves the character traits which Sitting Bull described. Helping others is a major aspect of the warrior lifestyle. It is part of your duty as a warrior. Street punks fight, but they are not warriors. Being able to fight is only a small part of the path of the warrior.

34

Violence is easy to escalate, hard to de-escalate.
Harland Cleveland

This is a very wise statement for every warrior to consider. Arguments can easily escalate into violent encounters, especially when emotions are heated. Fuses are even shorter when drugs or alcohol are involved. You should handle arguments and disagreements extremely carefully. It is important that you discern the personality, spirit and intention of the parties involved. Once circumstances escalate to the point of getting physical, it is extremely hard to calm everyone down.

Most people don't seem to comprehend the seriousness of a physical encounter and how quickly a simple argument can evolve into pushing and shoving, which then can explode into a more serious situation than anyone involved could imagine. Warriors do understand how serious fighting is and the damage that can be done to the human body, even by untrained men. They know that they should do everything possible to de-escalate the situation because once it is on, the stakes get much higher.

Look at arguments and disputes as opportunities to use your verbal and mental self-defense skills. You should develop these skills just as you develop your physical skills. Become a master at defusing explosive situations. Learn the art of mediation. Remember that a soft answer turns away wrath. Stay calm and speak with authority, but at the same time, speak with a nonthreatening tone which lets everyone know that you are doing everything possible to avoid conflict. Remember self-defense involves more than being able to defend yourself physically.

35

If you are a serious warrior, you'll become a student of anatomy.
Forrest E. Morgan

Become a student of human anatomy. Learning how the human body works gives you valuable information that you need for your life on the path of the warrior. There are two reasons for this. First, if you understand the fundamental way that the body is put together, you will realize how important it is to protect your body. You will start to understand just how fragile the human body actually is. This will also give you valuable insight into which parts of the body need extra protection and why certain areas have to be carefully protected. There are some spots on the body where a knife wound would not be fatal and other spots where just a ¼ inch cut could cost you your life. This is important information to know.

The second reason that you should become a student of the human anatomy is the flip side of the coin. By studying how the body functions, and the structure of the body, you are better prepared to attack the body. Just as there are certain areas that need greater protection, there are also certain areas which are better targets. There are spots on the body that can withstand a hard punch or kick, and there are spots on the body where a punch or kick could be a fatal blow. Martial arts skills are dangerous skills, and not knowing the human anatomy or not realizing how fragile the body can be, can make martial arts even more dangerous. Practice safe and fight smart.

36

Whoso would be a man must be a nonconformist.
Emerson

The warrior is a nonconformist. He refuses to lower his standards or his code of ethics to please others. The fact that other men may consider this action or that action to be acceptable, means nothing to the warrior. He is not interested in conforming to the opinions of others. He is only interested in living up to his own standards which he sets for himself.

If the warrior was the type of man that simply went along with the crowd, he would not be so rare. Anyone can bend their standards to conform to the standards of the day, but it takes a real man to stand firm concerning his ethics when all other men are trying to convince him to conform to their way of thinking. The warrior has to not only have confidence in his own code of honor, but also has to have confidence in his ability to walk alone against the tide of public opinion.

This attitude of independence is what makes the warrior a rare man of honor. He does what he knows in his heart to be right, independent of what anyone else says or does. He refuses to play the game of situational ethics. His ethics are set in stone. Others may not be able to decipher his code or understand his way of thinking, but they know that the warrior is a man of principle. He is not a man that can be manipulated by popular opinion or moral fads. The true warrior is a true nonconformist and always has been.

37

If I do my duty, the rest will take care of itself.
George S. Patton

The above sentiment is echoed by sages and warriors alike throughout the centuries. You are responsible for fulfilling your duty, but you are not responsible for the outcome of fulfilling that responsibility. All you should concern yourself with is the question of what is your duty at the present moment; what is the right thing to do right now. Once you know the answer to this question, then you have to take action. The end result of that action is out of your control.

This is a never-ending cycle. You decide what is right and what your duty is, and then you take action. Minute by minute, hour by hour, and day by day, this cycle repeats. You just continue to respond to the circumstances which present themselves to you. The hard part of this is deciding what your duty is and then having the courage to follow through and take action.

Here is where your character training comes into play. You have to know how to distinguish between right and wrong. You have to understand what your duty is as a warrior. These are decisions you have to make according to your code of ethics. Nobody can make these decisions for you. You and you alone, are responsible for the decisions that you make. Do what is right, and leave the outcome to God.

This brings us to the question of, "How do you know what your duty is?" Study and meditation on the ideals of warriorhood will answer this for you. Each warrior must find the answers to this question on his own. Just focus on what is right.

38

Your greatest weapon is in your enemy's mind.
Buddha

During the 17th and 18th centuries, pirates terrorized the waters of the Caribbean. It was a common practice for these pirates to use psychological warfare on the ships that they attacked. This was the main purpose of the famous skull and crossbones flags that we associate with pirates today. These flags were meant to instill terror into the minds of the sailors aboard the other ship, and weaken their resolve to fight back once they were attacked. Pirates attacked the minds of their enemies first and foremost.

This is a common strategy in battle and has been employed, probably since the first men fought each other. It is even used today in sporting events. If you can defeat your enemy mentally, you own him. Once he allows fear or anger to enter his mind, he is primed for defeat. He is no longer thinking rationally, but allowing his emotions to control his actions. When he gets to this point, he will make a mistake, and then it is up to you to take advantage of that mistake.

There is also another, less violent side to psychological warfare which the pirates used. They were hopeful that their fear tactics would enable them to achieve their goals without having to resort to actual combat. This should be your goal also. Attacking the enemy's mind should not only be your greatest weapon, but your first line of defense. Learn to manipulate your enemy's mind in order to resolve things without having to resort to actual combat. Avoid having to fight by learning how to defeat your enemy mentally. The peaceful victory is always more satisfying and safer.

39

We are what we repeatedly do.
Excellence is not an act, but a habit.
Aristotle

Do you want to be a man of honor, integrity and character? Then you have to act like a man of honor, integrity and character. Not just once and a while, not just when you are in a good mood, not just around people who you consider important, but all the time. You have to get into the habit of living a life full of honor. It doesn't just happen automatically. You have to practice it and work at it. Sometimes you have to just plain grit your teeth and do it despite your feelings, until the time when acting with honor and integrity becomes automatic.

Aristotle also tells us that excellence is an art form and that it is acquired by training and repetition. You do not do the right thing because you have virtue, but rather you have virtue because you do the right thing. Your actions and intentions form your character. Later, when your character has been formed and becomes a habit, it determines your actions.

The warrior must be careful to make his actions and intentions right. He has to make a habit out of this until he has perfected his character. Once he has begun to perfect his character, acts of honor and integrity come naturally, without conscious thought. When you get to this point, living a life of excellence will become your nature. Your actions determine who you become.

40

Don't assume your foe will be merciful.
Dirk Skinner

People who go through life without any training in self-defense techniques or without any means of self-defense at all, are either gambling on never being the victim of a predator or hoping that when and if they do run into a predator, he has mercy on them. This is a pretty big gamble in today's world. The violent crime statistics today are staggering. Violent street gangs are increasing in number daily and are becoming more brazen and violent.

I live in a fairly sheltered location, and yet I can take a walk just a few blocks from my house, any night of the week, and run into punks dealing drugs. I am not someone who predators would look at and think, "Now there's an easy target," yet I have had punks give me a hard time in our public park. Don't kid yourself on the odds of never having to deal with someone with less than honorable intentions, and when you do, you had better not be banking on that person's conscience and mercy to save you.

The national news has covered several instances where predators have attacked 85 and 90 year old men and women, not just taking their money, but violently punching them in the face over and over – 90 years old! And people are walking around hoping that these type people will somehow have mercy on them if they are attacked? Don't count on it! You will receive no mercy; you had better be prepared.

41

Don't teach undesirable people.
Masaaki Hatsumi

In the past, martial arts masters refused to teach their art to just anyone who came through the door requesting to learn from them. Their arts were considered sacred, as were the dojos where they taught their students. The martial arts skills and philosophy that they taught were passed down from master to student over the years. Most of the teachers did not make their living by teaching martial arts. Gichin Funakoshi, for example, was a school teacher, and taught martial arts on the side.

It is totally different in today's world. The martial arts have become big business. There are dojos everywhere you look, and most will accept anyone who has the financial ability to pay their monthly fee and who will sign a long term contract. It is all about money for many people today. No one is turned away, and if they are turned away at one dojo, there are plenty of others who will accept them. This is not the way that it should be.

When you teach someone true martial arts techniques, it is the same as giving them a weapon and showing them how to use it. Sure there are plenty of dojos which are strictly for sport, but they are also teaching dangerous information. Someone's character should be discerned before they are given such weapons. A friend of mine, who happens to be a policeman, told me that dojos have financial concerns and can't afford to turn away paying students. My response was that, as a warrior, you have to put what is right before what is profitable. Always put what is right before what is profitable. Don't teach undesirable students the art of war.

42

Let not the fruit of action
be your motive to act.
The Bhagavad Gita

The motivation behind your actions should be to fulfill your duty as a warrior. If you see that a course of action is the right course to take, you should take it. Don't be swayed to change your course because of the possible consequences, if you know that you are right. If you see a lady getting mugged on the street, you should step in. It would be wrong if you saw this happening and yet did nothing because you don't want to get involved. On the other hand, it would also be wrong for you to step in because you are interested in getting a reward or getting on the nightly news.

Your motive for doing the right thing should be the simple fact that it is the right thing to do, period. Don't let the outcome of doing the right thing trouble you. Be concerned with doing your duty, and let God take care of the outcome. All you can do is live as you should and take the right action when you determine what that action is. You have no control over the outcome.

Although doing the right thing without apprehension concerning the end result is a basic part of the warrior lifestyle, it is not enough. Your intentions have to be right. Your motives need to be pure. Remember, you must perfect your character, and your thoughts and intentions are a big part of the equation. Don't allow wrong intentions or dishonorable motivations to tarnish good actions. Make things right, inside and out. Do the right thing, for the right reason, at the right time. It has to be right on the inside, before it can be right on the outside.

43

Deprived of all else, one remains undisgraced if still endowed with strength of character.
Tiruvalluvar

Many things can be taken away from you in this life. You can lose your loved ones. Your home can be lost. Money, possessions, titles, health, can all be taken away with hardly any advance notice. Although it is unimaginable in our country, you could also lose your freedom. In fact, there is very little in your life that can't be taken away from you in one form or another. One of the few things that can't be taken away is your character.

No one can take away your character, your honor, or your integrity. You have total control over these things. Whatever else you may lose, Tiruvalluvar tells us that you will remain undisgraced if you hold on to your character. This doesn't mean that you can't lose your character, integrity or honor. You can certainly lose your integrity and honor, and your character can be tarnished. You must be careful and work to make sure that this doesn't happen.

Notice that I said no one can *take* these things away from you, but they can be lost. You make this decision yourself. You are the deciding factor as far as whether or not you maintain your character, honor and integrity. As a warrior, you have to ensure that your character is always intact. Don't lower your expectations concerning your character for anyone or anything. Make the hard decisions according to your unyielding code of ethics which sets you apart from other men. Maintain your character, honor and integrity at all cost. This is your duty. This is the lifestyle of the warrior.

44

Deal with a dangerous situation while it is safe. Eliminate what is vicious before it becomes destructive.
Lao Tzu

One of my favorite books is the *Tao Te Ching*. This book is packed full of wisdom. In the *Tao*, Lao Tzu tells us that it is best to deal with dangerous situations while they are still safe. This is exactly what the warrior should attempt to do when things start to get heated between other people. We all realize that a physical encounter can be a very dangerous and destructive situation. Things can get violent very quickly.

Your duty as a warrior is to try your best to stop circumstances from getting to that point. Take control before tempers start to boil. Deal with the situation and handle it with your psychological skills. Attack your opponent's mind without him ever knowing that is what you are doing. Manipulate the situation without allowing others to see that you are in control. Taking these subtle actions before things get to the point of no return can eliminate a vicious threat before anyone else even recognizes that there was imminent danger.

Train yourself to recognize a dangerous situation before it occurs. Don't allow your pride to get in the way of your victory. Sun Tzu taught that the best victory is won without fighting. This is what he was talking about. Learn to fight using subtle techniques, so subtle that your enemy doesn't even realize he has been in a battle, much less that he has been completely defeated. These techniques come from using your mind, not your muscles, but they can be just as effective.

45

I wasn't born knowing what I teach you. Being fond of the past, I sought it through diligence.
Confucius

Nobody is born with the wisdom of a sage or the character traits of a true warrior. These are things which have to be developed over time. Not only does it take time to develop the character traits that are an essential part of the warrior lifestyle, but it also takes a lot of work and perseverance. You don't just decide one day that you are going to live the lifestyle of the warrior, and all of a sudden, these traits magically become a part of you.

It takes a lot of discipline to perfect your character, to make the traits of the warrior your own. As I have said before, the warrior lifestyle is a journey, not a destination. Just as you struggle when learning any new endeavor, you will have your challenges on your path to warriorhood. No one said that the lifestyle of the warrior is easy. It is a struggle, at least at first, until these qualities are internalized in your spirit.

The trick to perfecting your character or your martial arts skills, is staying on the path. Don't give up because you fall short or because you have something that is threatening to block your path. Just as your muscles will not grow without the challenge of increased resistance, your character will not improve without using it in the real world. Anyone can sail a ship when the weather is calm, the test comes when the winds pick up and the storm clouds roll in around you. Be diligent in your quest to become a true warrior.

46

Whatever you think,
be sure it is what you think.
T. S. Eliot

Independence is an important trait of the warrior. Many times the warrior's view, whether on ethics or actions that have to be taken, differ from that of the average person. He is an independent spirit and must have the courage to stand by both his thoughts and his convictions. The warrior shouldn't allow himself to be swayed by the voice of public opinion or outside pressures from people who do not share the same ethics as he does.

A warrior's thoughts have to be his own. He must determine what is right and wrong by the strict code of ethics which he has set for himself. Nobody else can do that for him. Very few people share his convictions concerning right and wrong, good and evil, or honor and integrity, therefore he must think for himself. If you allow others to influence your thinking, instead of thinking rationally for yourself, you have given away part of your freedom, the freedom to think and decide for yourself.

The majority of people in our society today do just that. They allow the government, the news media, the schools, or their family members to think for them. They are too lazy to take the time and think about a subject rationally and then make up their own mind about the issue. It is much easier for them to allow the radio shows or television hosts to tell them what to believe. The problem is that this is also much more dangerous. Others control you when you allow them to think for you. Don't allow others to play mind games with you. Think for yourself. Make sure that what you believe is what you believe.

47

Every man has three characters – that which he exhibits, that which he has, and that which he thinks he has.
Alphonse Karr

This is a pretty interesting statement and I would agree that it applies to the majority of the people in the world today. You only get to see what people allow you to see, as far as their character goes. It takes only seconds, in many cases, to see that someone is lacking in character, integrity or honor, but it can take years to actually determine whether or not someone's character is upstanding.

The majority of people will act one way in public and another way in private. They put on a charade in public so others will think highly of them. Personally, they may think they are of the highest morale character, but they really never stop and deeply examine their character or beliefs to truly understand themselves. Therefore, most people have what Alphonse Karr describes as three characters, but this is not truly accurate.

In truth every man has only one character; the other two "characters" are only charades. They are nothing more than insincere actions and thoughts which deceive both the public and the individual himself. This should not describe the warrior. The warrior must strive to make these "three characters" one and the same. He must not act one way in public and one way in private. Sincerity is essential. He must see himself as he truly is and endeavor to perfect his one true character daily. Never deceive yourself.

48

Having the idea is not living the reality.
Rumi

In our world, which has become dominated by the internet and all of the various on-line entertainments, many people find themselves living a type of fantasy life. They have "friends" on-line which they have never met. They carry on conversations with people who may or may not be real, and believe that they have numerous friends, but when they meet someone face-to-face, they find that the social skills which work so well for them online, don't really transfer into the real world. There is a big difference in the real world and the little fantasy world which they have created.

In the same way, many people read books on the subject of martial arts and watch videos on how to defend themselves. Many go to dojos to learn how to defend themselves with the skills of a true martial artist, but never have used their "skills" beyond the safety of the choreographed moves which most dojos practice for their self-defense training. Mentally they believe that they know what they are doing when it comes to self-defense, but do they really?

As Rumi tells us, having an idea about something is not the same thing as living the reality. Sparring in a safe environment with a familiar partner, is much different from a no rules street fight where your life is on the line and the other person is trying his best to do as much damage to your body as possible. You can't live your life in your own little bubble and expect to be prepared for real life when you finally get the courage to go out into the world. Train for authenticity and be ready for the reality of the streets.

49

If you live in the river you should understand the crocodile.
Indian Proverb

The mind of the predator is so foreign to the majority of people walking around today, that they can't even imagine how predators think. You hear them make comments such as, "People are all the same," or "People are just people." They have no concept about the mindset of someone who is capable of committing murder or assaulting an elderly lady.

The criminal mind is different. People are not all the same. Predators have different values than the average person. They don't value human life the way the normal person does. Expecting someone, who does not value human life, to act the same as the average person or to behave as an upstanding citizen, is absurd. There are people out there who would kill you over pocket change and not give your passing a second thought. Predators are different!

If you live by the river, you need to understand the ways of the crocodile. Even if you only visit the river occasionally, you still should understand the dangers which it holds. You need to know what to look for and how to avoid those dangers. You need to know how to respond and what to do should you come face to face with the dangerous predators that live on the river.

If you live in an environment where these type people live, you need to understand who they are and how they think. My book, *Wicked Wisdom*, can be a great help where this is concerned. Don't be caught off guard by a naive world view. Not everyone you run into is going to be just another nice person.

50

Those who play with cats
must expect to be scratched.
Cervantes

Have you ever played with a cat using a string or some other toy? If so, you know that no matter how careful you are, you usually get scratched. That is just the nature of cats. They are not careful about where their claws strike. They just instinctively claw at things, and many times they hit you instead of the toy.

The same principle goes for people. If you are going to hang around with thugs, street punks, or people of low character, be prepared to be scratched. That is just their nature. There is no honor among thieves, and there is no true friendship among people of low character. I know that this statement will be offensive to some people, but it is true. You cannot trust people who do not esteem virtue and character, and it is a mistake, many times a dangerous mistake, to put your trust in them.

All of the sages throughout history tell us that it is vitally important to choose the right people to associate with and to allow to be a part of your life. Choosing the wrong people to be "friends" with, people of low character, can cause major problems for you, and at the least, will not help you on your path of warriorship. The wise man should choose to associate only with those who will help him on his journey, those who have wisdom to share with him. Why would you choose to associate with someone who has nothing positive to offer you, but potentially could cause you much heartache and trouble? The man who associates with the sage becomes wise; the man who associates with the cat gets scratched. Think about this.

51

Be your friend's true friend.
The Havamal

The true warrior is the best friend you could possibly imagine finding in your lifetime. He understands the value of true friendship, as well as understanding the difference in a friend and an acquaintance. Because he is a man who takes his word, his honor and his character seriously, he is the kind of friend that you can count on to be there when the chips are down. He is not a fair weather friend. It is in his nature to stand by his friends in times of trouble and to go to bat for his friends when they need him.

His understanding of what a friend should be is far beyond that of most men. Once you are truly his friend, you have a friend for life. Moreover, you have a friend with character, honor and integrity, one who will help you on your journey, and not be a hindrance. He is a friend who appreciates the type of lifestyle that you are working so hard to manifest in your life. The warrior is a friend by the true definition of the word. He will stand side by side with you, should you need his aid. The whole idea of turning his back on his friend is so repulsive to the warrior, that the thought of it never enters his mind.

During your life, you will have many acquaintances, but very few real friends. Don't get the two confused. There is a tremendous difference in both the definitions and the reality of the two. Once you have a true friend, you should be a true friend in return. Your friends should know that you are there for them, no matter what. They should know what it means to have a warrior as a friend. Anything less is dishonorable.

52

Snakes follow the way of serpents.
Japanese Proverb

Snakes follow the way of serpents, and fools follow the way of fools. I have talked a lot about how the warrior should act; now let's look at the antithesis of the warrior, the fool. There are characteristics which define the fool, just as there are characteristics which define the warrior. The sages tell us that fools are full of pride and find pleasure in evil deeds. They are ungrateful, unintelligent, short-sighted, and always in the majority.

Fools are not fond of study, but rather they waste their time in other people's business, and participate in malicious gossip. Though they have a shocking lack of wisdom, they esteem themselves as wise. They refuse to listen to advice from the wise, but find pleasure in airing their own opinions. Although the fool may acquire knowledge, he never acquires understanding. Hypocrisy is the trademark of the fool, he is rarely sincere.

These unwise men believe whatever they are told, except when it comes to real wisdom. They are easily led astray and make easy targets for predators and swindlers. Speaking without thought is common with these men. Fools are quick to offer an insult, and even quicker to become angry and willing to fight. The *Book of Proverbs* says that fools die for lack of judgment.

These traits do not paint the picture of a warrior. The warrior lifestyle is a completely different road than the one that the fool travels. If you find that any of these traits are present in your life, it is time to make some changes. Think about this.

53

To generalize is to be an idiot.
William Blake

There are very few statements which are absolute. Things are not always black and white; in fact most things are not black and white. Therefore it is unwise to make generalizations, but every day there are examples of people who make absolute statements in our media. One of the statements often heard, especially in our schools today is that there is never any reason for violence; violence never solves anything.

The word never implies that it never happens. The people who make such statements usually don't believe them themselves. Does anyone believe that violence has never solved anything? It certainly has served to save many lives. World War II is a perfect example. Yes, many lives were lost during World War II, but think about how many more lives would have been lost without a violent intervention.

Self-defense, many times involves violence, and I can assure you that there is a very good reason for violence when you are being attacked and your life is on the line. Furthermore, I doubt that these same people who state that there is never any reason for violence, would not fight back if they were being attacked and their life was being threatened.

Don't make blanket statements. To anyone who is thinking rationally, generalizations demonstrate, at the very least, a lack of thought, and in the worst case scenario, a lack of intelligence, neither which is fitting for a warrior. Think rationally and think before you speak. Generalizations are not the way of the warrior.

54

Reading makes a full man –
Meditation makes a profound man.
Benjamin Franklin

Everyone should read as much as possible and learn about various subjects. Today, with the amount of information available on the internet and in the book stores, you can learn virtually anything that you may want to know just by taking the time to read. It is important that you continually increase your learning. Never lose your curiosity and your love of learning. As Benjamin Franklin stated, this will make you a full man, but reading is not enough.

The act of reading something alone can be as fruitless as mindlessly staring at a television screen while your mind is somewhere else. You have to engage your mind and focus while you read. Be in the moment. Meditate on the information that you are studying. Don't just skim it, but rather understand it. Understand the principles behind what you are reading and be able to apply those principles to your life.

This applies to everything that you do. When you are learning martial arts, focus on what you are doing at the time. Do not let your mind wonder off to some other subject. Be in the moment. Focus on the Now. Don't just go through motions, but learn the principles behind the techniques. Once you understand the principles, the rest will make sense to you. Meditate on what you have learned and visualize yourself using the techniques perfectly. Without a deep understanding, you have not mastered the information or the technique.

55

A door must either be open or shut.
French Proverb

Just as a door must either be open or closed; your actions must be honorable or dishonorable. In our culture, we play pretty loose with our speech. A door may be almost closed, and yet we say that the door is closed, when in actuality, the door is a half inch from really being closed. By a strict definition, the door is not really closed, it is slightly open. It is almost closed, but "almost closed" is still open. Now we could start discussing how close to being closed the door is, but that doesn't change the fact that the door is, in truth, still not closed.

The same principle goes for your actions. Each action is either an honorable action or it isn't. What you say is either true or it is not true. The bottom line is it has to be one or the other. You may argue that an action is mostly honorable, or that a statement is mostly true, so overall it is honorable or true. Let's take a look at that point of view.

If you tell me a story, and it is all true but the ending, then that story is mostly true, but it still contains an untruth, therefore what you said is not true. It doesn't matter that most of it was true. It is either true or it is not true, just as a door is either open or not open. We could say, well it is 90% true, but who trusts someone who lies 10% of the time? Do you want to be known as someone who tells the truth most of the time, or someone who's word is his honor? Do you want to be someone who acts honorably most of the time, or someone who acts honorably, period? Honor is not black and white, but your actions are either honorable or dishonorable. Think about this.

56

To every man there opens a high way and a low way, and every man decides the way his soul will go.
John Oxenham

Every man has the freedom to choose how he will live his life, as far as his character, honor and integrity is concerned. Even those in slavery or in prison have the choice of how they will conduct themselves in their present situations. This is a choice that no one can take from you. You choose the direction that your spirit will take on your journey. The choices vary, but overall, it boils down to whether or not you are willing to do what it takes to live a life of excellence or will you take the easy road, the road that the majority chooses to travel.

The low road, or the easy road, is actually very wide and has multiple routes. Some of the routes are totally unconcerned with morals or ethics in any way. Other routes pay a bit of attention to certain character traits, but ignore others. Each route on the low road has various philosophies about how those who travel this road will live their lives, but they all have one thing in common, they shy away from the excellence of the high road.

The high road is a narrow path and is a harder road to travel. There are not multiple paths on this road. There is only the path of excellence. This road is paved with character, honor and integrity, and those who travel it know that to stray from this path, is to leave the high road and move towards a lower way of life. This road is not too crowded because most people choose not to travel it, but in the end, the high road leads to a much better destination than the low road. Which road will you choose?

57

When we show our respect for other living things, they respond with respect for us.
Arapaho Proverb

Showing respect for all living things is a principle of Native American philosophy. The Native Americans taught that all things have a spirit and therefore all things should be shown respect. The Arapaho proverb above states that we should show respect for other living things, and they will respond with respect for us. It does not say that you have to actually respect everyone.

There is a difference between showing someone respect and actually respecting that person. You may think that everyone deserves respect, but that is not quite right. Everyone deserves to be treated with respect, but everyone is not deserving of respect. There is a big difference. Whether or not someone deserves respect depends on their character and behavior. Whether or not you treat someone with respect depends on you doing the right thing as a warrior. See the difference?

You can treat someone in a respectful manner even if you have no respect for that person for whatever reason. Respect is not a right or a privilege; it is something that you earn by the way that you choose to live your life. Your character determines the amount of respect you deserve. Your decorum dictates the respectful manner in which you treat all others. Be deserving of respect, and be honorable enough to show respect to others, whether they deserve it or not. Showing others respect is akin to being courteous, and being courteous to others is simply a part of the warrior lifestyle. Think about this.

58

Don't easily trust anyone on this earth because there are all kinds.
Bruce Lee

During your lifetime you are going to run across a lot of different kinds of people, and the sages have always taught that the majority of the people that you meet will not be people of the highest character. People are different; they don't all have the same character traits or the same standards. Many of the people you meet will not think twice about lying to you in their business dealings. As amazing as it seems to the warrior, a lot of people lie, cheat and steal whenever it suits their purpose.

Traits such as these are foreign to the warrior and his lifestyle, but he must be aware that they are common in the world. The way of the warrior has always been rare, but is even more so in today's society. Knowing this, it is wise to be careful concerning who you trust. As the Russian proverb goes, "Trust but verify." Don't just blindly trust everyone that you do business with in this world. If you do, I can assure you that you will be sorely disappointed.

The warrior must be able to discern the honest man from the dishonest man. See things as they really are and look beyond the charade. Be prepared to be tested by people who will look you square in the eye and lie through their teeth without blinking or missing a beat. This kind of person is becoming more and more common, and you will have to learn how to deal with them. Be prepared to deal with those who don't live by a code of honor, and deal with their lack of integrity with the same high standards in which you deal with all people.

59

Hold yourself responsible for a higher standard than anyone else expects of you. Never excuse yourself.
Henry Ward Beecher

To the warrior, laws are pretty much worthless. Laws are for men of low character who need someone else to keep them in line with the threat of punishment. This is not to say that warriors do not have to obey the laws of the land, at least most of the time. What it does mean is that the warrior's code of ethics is actually stricter than any law of the land. His standards require him to keep a closer watch on his actions than any law could.

The warrior holds himself to a higher standard than anyone else expects of him, just as Henry Ward Beecher suggests that you should do. He doesn't bend his "rules" as one does with discretionary laws such as speed limits, etc. For this reason, he finds most laws useless. The true man of character doesn't need laws in order to do what he should. He simply does what's right regardless of whether or not there is a law to guide him.

Moreover, even if there were no laws, the warrior would still live the same lifestyle of honor and integrity. The point here is that the warrior sets his own law. That law is his code of honor or code of ethics. He decides what is right and what is just, and lives accordingly. You may be thinking if everyone did that we would have anarchy, and you would be exactly right. Everyone is not a man of honor. That is why we have to have laws - for lesser men who will not discipline themselves.

60

It is better to be a tiger for one day than a sheep for a thousand years.
Tibetan Maxim

This is an interesting maxim from Tibet. It is better to be a tiger for one day than a sheep for a thousand years. Most people today are sheep. This is not a derogatory statement, but rather a statement of fact. Sheep go through life pretty much oblivious to what is happening around them. They eat, drink, sleep, and follow their shepherd wherever he desires to lead them. A sheep is a peaceful animal and presents no threat to other animals; it just kind of goes through life on auto-pilot.

The tiger, on the other hand, roams the jungle with confidence and awareness. Tigers have no shepherd to protect them or guide them to food and water. A tiger is a self-sufficient animal capable of not only providing its own food, but of also defending itself against pretty much any threat. Tigers are proficient killing machines when they have to be. Their confidence shows in their unflinching gaze. They set their own law in the jungle.

The Tibetan maxim above tells us that it is better to live like a tiger, even if it is only for a short time, than it is to live many years as a sheep. The warrior has much more in common with the tiger than he does with the sheep. He is confident and independent. He is self-sufficient and fierce. Warriors roam the streets of the jungle knowing that they can handle most anything that comes their way. It is better to be a warrior for a year than a sheep for 100 years.

61

Never exchange a good conscience for the good will of others, or to avoid their ill-will.
Charles Simmons

The warrior should never compromise on his values. Don't negotiate your honor in an attempt to keep others satisfied. People who don't appreciate that you are a man of honor and that you live by high standards, will not think any higher of you if you bend your rules for them. Oh, they will act appreciative; they will pat you on the back and tell you what a good decision you made. But inside, they will only be thinking that they were able to manipulate you and that your values and integrity are situational and not set in stone.

If they ever had any respect for you, they won't after they see you compromise on something which you professed to hold so dear. Deep inside, in places where they will never allow you to go, they will feel that, when it comes down to it, you are a hypocrite who says one thing, but does another. You may have temporarily won their good will or kept them from being upset with you, but I assure you, this will only be temporary.

It will not be long until they want something else. What will you do next time? Will you compromise your honor and integrity again? How will your argument stand up when you tell them that you can't do what they ask because it is against your code of ethics, and they respond, with "that sure didn't stop you the last time?" Compromising on your standards is like a boulder rolling down the mountain side; once you start down that slope, it becomes hard to stop, and even harder to get back to where you were. Don't compromise where your honor or integrity is concerned.

62

With sincerity, there is virtue.
Shinto Maxim

A person can't really be virtuous without being sincere. Without sincerity, there is no honor or integrity; there is only a charade, played out for others to see, and for the benefit of the actor. Many people want to be seen as having these virtuous character traits without having to put forth the effort that is required to actually have them be a part of their lives. Their agenda is not to perfect their character, but rather to perfect their appearance. They are interested in all of the benefits that come from having an honorable name, but not in the discipline that it takes to become honorable.

The key ingredient that is missing in these people is sincerity. They are not sincere, and without sincerity, there is no virtue, even if there appears to be virtue. The warrior must be able to distinguish between a person of virtue and the person who only appears virtuous. Unfortunately, the majority of the people you meet will fit into the latter category. Many people love to read and talk about honor, integrity, and character, but they don't really apply these virtues to their own life.

Don't be like the person who only appears honorable; be honorable. Be sincere in your quest to live the warrior lifestyle. Make these virtues a part of who you are, not because of the external benefits, but because of the internal benefits that come from being a man of virtue. Take your life seriously and take your character seriously. If you don't, you will falter when the chips are down and your back is against the wall. You must be sincere.

63

Embrace the snake and it will bite you.
Bulgarian Proverb

There is an old Japanese folk tale about the farmer and the snake which would serve you well to remember. The farmer was out working on his farm one day, getting ready for the winter snows to set in. It was already cold and snow was on the ground. While doing his chores, he came across a snake lying in the snow, nearly frozen to death. Feeling benevolent, the farmer wrapped the snake in his coat and took it inside his home to see if he could save the poor creature.

The farmer laid the snake on the floor in front of the fireplace to warm it up and see if he could revive it. He checked on it often to see if it was going to live or not. As the snake started to show a bit of life, the farmer went into the kitchen to get some water for his new friend. Coming back into the room with the saucer of water, the farmer leaned over and placed the water in front of the snake. In a split second, the snake lunged out and bit the farmer in the neck, rendering a lethal dose of toxic venom.

As he lay on the floor, dying from the venomous bite, the farmer looked at the snake and asked, "Why did you kill me after I saved your life?" The snake coldly said, as it slithered away, "I can't help it, it's just my nature." Learn to judge the nature of others. There are many bad people out there who will take advantage of any help you offer, and then stab you in the back. Help others when you can, but be selective about who you help and what you get yourself into. See things as they really are.

64

Men flourish only for a moment.
Homer

Nobody is promised tomorrow. All of the sages have taught that your time on this earth is very short; it goes by in a flash. From the earliest wisdom writings to the Native American and the samurai, every warrior culture knew the importance of using the time that you have on this earth wisely. This is even truer for the warrior because the warrior lives life on the edge, never knowing when duty may require him to put his life on the line, and when fate may dictate that his time here is finished.

Juvenal put it this way, "The short bloom of our brief life flies fast away. While we are calling for flowers and wine and women, old age is upon us." Time is extremely deceptive. While you go about your day to day routine, the sands of time continue to flow to the bottom of the hourglass. Knowing that you don't have all the time in the world, you should take pains to live right, today. Don't delay. If there is anything that you want to learn, study, or do with your life, do it now.

The samurai warriors recognized the importance of this in their lives. A samurai's daimyo, feudal lord for whom the samurai was employed, could require that the samurai warrior commit suicide at his will, and the samurai was obliged to do so. Samurai warriors understood, that because of their lifestyle, tomorrow was never guaranteed to them, therefore, they made sure that they were prepared for death. They lived their life by strict standards of honor, and they took life seriously. You are only here for a moment. Now is the time to live the warrior lifestyle; later may be too late.

65

People hate those who make them feel their own inferiority.
Lord Chesterfield

Have you ever noticed how, if a football team develops into a dynasty, everyone wants to see them get beat? This is because nobody likes to feel inferior to anyone else, and a team who has practiced, worked, and grabbed hold of excellence, makes those who have not, feel inferior. The same principle applies to individuals. Those who have developed their lives to the point of excellence, make others who have not, feel inferior, unless they are very careful about how they carry themselves.

The warrior should develop his life to the point of excellence, while at the same time living in such a way as to not make those who haven't, feel inferior. Yes, this is a tall order on both accounts. It is hard enough to live the life of the superior man, who has worked to develop his character through many hours of discipline and training, but once you start to feel that you are making progress, it can be even harder not to make others feel inferior. You have to watch what you say and how you treat those who are less inclined to live a life of honor.

How do you live a life of excellence and honor without making others feel inferior? The answer lies in respect. You have to treat them with respect, even if you don't really respect their lifestyle choices. This is not being hypocritical. It is simply treating others as you would have them treat you. Inside, you may know that men of honor, who live the warrior lifestyle, deserve more respect and reverence, but this fact doesn't mean that you shouldn't treat others respectfully.

66

It is easier to prevent bad habits than to break them.
Benjamin Franklin

Part of the duty of the warrior is to develop good habits in every area of his life, spiritually, mentally and physically. Essentially, the development of the right habits is what *Warrior Wisdom* is all about. Honor, character, and integrity have to be practiced and studied until they become a habit. In the same way, your workouts and your meditation time have to become a habit; they have to become a part of who you are, not just something that you do.

As demanding as this duty may sound, it is much easier to develop these traits and make them your predominant habits, than it is to allow bad habits to take root and then to try to break them. Bad habits will have to be dealt with in order to live the lifestyle of the warrior. Just as noxious weeds are contrary to your goals if you are a gardener, many bad habits are directly contrary to the qualities that you need to foster on the path of the warrior. Therefore these bad habits have to be rooted out.

If you have ever done any gardening, you know how much easier it is to put down mulch or fabric to stop weeds from ever growing in your garden, than it is to allow weeds to grow for weeks and then try to get rid of them. Once the weeds have developed strong roots, they are extremely hard to eliminate. The same principle applies to bad habits. Prevent them before they develop strong roots in your life.

67

What is not increased diminishes.
Rumi

I have said many times that no matter how far you paddle up the river, when you quit paddling, you start to go back to where you were. This is a natural law. The current of the river is constantly flowing down the river to the ocean. If you are working hard to paddle to a certain spot up the river, when you stop paddling, the current is still flowing, and it will take you right back where you started.

What's more, it takes absolutely no effort on your part to go back to where you started; all you have to do is sit there and do nothing and through the natural flow of the river, you will find that, in no time at all, you end up back at the beginning. The only way to stop this from happening is to keep paddling. The river current doesn't take a day off. If you aren't working to maintain the position that you have achieved, or working to continue to paddle even further up the river, you will drift back down the river. This is just the way it is.

The same principle applies to your martial arts training and your character training. You may have made great strides towards becoming who you want to be on the path of the warrior, but if you rest on your laurels, you will find that you start to lose what you have worked so hard for. It takes work to maintain your skills; it takes nothing but inaction for those skills to diminish. What you don't use, you lose. What is not increased diminishes; there is no standing still. You are either moving forward or backward, moving towards your goals or away from your goals. You choose.

68

When you arise in the morning, give thanks for the morning light, for your life and strength. Give thanks for your food and the joy of living. If you see no reason for giving thanks, the fault lies in yourself.
Tecumseh

Spirituality has always been a part of the warrior lifestyle, and so have the character traits of gratitude and appreciation. Tecumseh tells us that each morning you should be thankful for all of your blessings. Be thankful for your health, your family, for having enough food and water, for living in a peaceful, free society, or simply for the fact that you are alive.

There are any number of things in which you can be thankful for in your life. Even if you are running into hard times at the present moment, you can find much to be thankful for, just meditate on the blessings that you have in your life. Tecumseh certainly did not have a life of leisure at the time he taught this. He was at war for the very existence of his people, and yet he continued his teaching with the statement that if you don't see a reason to be thankful, the fault lies in yourself.

If you find that you have a bitter attitude toward life and the things which are unfolding in your life, it is time to do some soul searching. The samurai taught that we should cleanse our hearts morning and night. Don't allow bitterness to reside in your heart or mind. Meditating on the things in your life which you appreciate is one way to keep resentment and bitterness out of your heart. We all, as Tecumseh taught, have things to be thankful for in our lives. Be thankful – it is the way of the warrior.

69

**Ikken hisatsu – one punch kills – is the essence of karate.
Put everything – your whole life – into one punch.**
Masami Tsuruoka

In our politically correct society, we don't hear the phrase "one punch – one kill" much anymore. You are much more likely to hear things such as strike here, there, and here, and you will score a point, but if you draw blood you will be disqualified. Martial arts have become more of a sport than what they were meant to be, which is a way to defend yourself against a deadly assault. They were never meant to be a sport or a fun activity for kids. The martial arts were deadly serious; they weren't some sort of game.

Many of today's martial artists see traditional arts as either strictly a form of art or just boring and outdated. They neglect the fact that when these arts originated, they were not for competition, sport, or hobby; they were for combat. The fact that many people see traditional martial arts as outdated simply shows their lack of understanding of these arts. Has the art of hand-to-hand combat changed so much that old techniques are only useful for tournaments?

The old techniques were not developed to look flashy or to show one's flexibility. They were developed to destroy one's enemy as efficiently as possible. The "kiai" of the warrior was not originally meant to be yelled as loud and as long as possible to earn points in a tournament, but rather to focus all of one's energy into a single blow, a blow meant to kill. Don't confuse a sport black belt with the black belt of a true warrior; there is a huge difference between the two.

70

Who with the wolf associates, to howl learns.
Bulgarian Proverb

I have talked a lot about the importance of being careful about who you associate with and being careful about ensuring that you have quality friends. If you walk with wise men, you will become wise. If you walk with men of honor, you will begin to become more like those men. You see where this is going? You begin to pick up the habits of those people that you associate with on a regular basis. If you desire to increase your wisdom or improve your character, associate with wise men of good character. The opposite is also true.

Just as associating with good men will help you become a better man, associating with bad men will make it harder for you to reach your goals for the warrior lifestyle. You will start to pick up the behavior of those around you whether those behaviors are good or bad. The more you are around people who are doing things that you once would never consider doing yourself, the more you become desensitized concerning those behaviors. Your overall attitude changes and it becomes easier to compromise your standards.

This is the reason that it is vitally important to carefully select who you hang around with and who you consider to be your friend. Think of your friends and acquaintances in terms of do they help you attain your goals or do they hinder the attainment of your goals. Why would you want to continue a relationship with someone who is continually throwing roadblocks in front of you on the path that you have decided to walk? Choose your acquaintances carefully, and your friends even more carefully.

71

Thatch your roof before rainy weather; dig your well before you are thirsty.
Chinese Proverb

You have to be prepared for what you may have to deal with long before you actually find yourself face to face with the challenge. The warrior can't wait until he is face to face with an attacker before he thinks about whether or not he is in shape to defend himself. You don't wait until the ruffian is at your door. When the thug has entered your space, you cannot call "time-out," stretch, and warm up. You have to be ready. This is why warrior training is vital. You never know when you will have a situation for which you must already be prepared.

If you wait until you are thirsty, and have no water, before you think about digging your well, you may likely die of thirst. If you wait until the storm comes before you fix your roof, you are assured that your roof will not protect you from the rain. If you wait until you have no choice but to fight for your life, to hone your martial arts skills, you may very well lose your life. You have to prepare for tomorrow's battle today.

Think ahead and plan for the future. Be disciplined. Don't start thinking that your training doesn't matter because you may never actually need it. Today may be the day that your training saves your life or the life of your loved ones. Train hard, don't put it off. Make sure that you are prepared for whatever may come. Being unprepared for whatever reason, is simply leaving your life to chance. This is not the way of the warrior. Be a warrior – be prepared.

72

Defeat is a state of mind; no one is ever defeated until defeat has been accepted as a reality.
Bruce Lee

Nothing is over until it is completely over, and you can't be defeated until you declare defeat. My friend, Don, is a retired lawman who worked in a large border town. Don has many colorful stories, but the one that I am about to tell you really demonstrates this quote on defeat by Bruce Lee.

Don had been called to this bar late one night, as lawmen often are, to take care of a bit of business. Business concluded, he was on his way out the door, headed home, when a huge guy in a cowboy hat and boots, blocked his path with his leg. This guy looked at Don with a cold stare and said, tonight, I'm going to kick your ass. Don said that by the look of this man, he knew that he meant it, and he also knew that he could get the job done. The following was Don's response.

You may kick my ass tonight, but tomorrow night I will be back with a deputy, and if we can't set things right, I will be back the next night with two more deputies. We have 465 lawmen in this county, and I will come back as many nights as it takes to make things right, and then, on top of that, you will be going to jail. The man simply removed his leg and let Don pass.

Then Don told me, "You know Bohdi, the Creed of the Texas Ranger is what I believe in, no man in the wrong can beat a man in the right that just keeps coming." Defeat is a state of mind. Losing one battle does not equal a lost war. You decide when to declare victory or defeat. Don't declare victory too soon, and don't declare defeat at all.

73

Never separate yourself from the Way of the Warrior.
Miyamoto Musashi

When one reads this statement written by Musashi so many years ago, the first thought is Musashi is just trying to say how great it is to be a warrior, but this statement takes on a deeper meaning once you really understand the way of the warrior. The way of the warrior should be the life that everyone lives. It is the way that human beings were meant to live. It means much more than just training physically in a martial art.

Departing from the way of the warrior is departing from the way of character, honor, and integrity. It is abandoning the spiritual connection which the warrior has with his Maker. Leaving this path means discarding your code of ethics and your sense of right and wrong. For those who separate from the way of the warrior, filial duty is no longer a priority in their lives. Self-discipline and self-reliance goes by the wayside.

Why would anyone want to separate from the way of the warrior, but then again, why doesn't everyone live the warrior lifestyle? The answer is that they do not have a true understanding of the benefits of this lifestyle. All they can see is the discipline that it takes to walk this path. They are shortsighted, not being able to see past their instant gratification. Warriors know that the training, discipline, and work it takes to live this lifestyle are worth it. They know that this lifestyle is not just something that they do, but is something that they are. You cannot separate yourself from something you are and live a fulfilled life. Stay on the path.

74

If your temper rises, withdraw your hand; if your hand rises, withdraw your temper.
Gojun Miyagi

Allowing your temper to control your actions is always a bad decision. This statement is even truer when it comes to physical confrontations. So many people believe that they become some kind of unstoppable force when they get angry and explode. For some reason the feeling that they get when they feel that rush of adrenaline through their body, translates in their minds to the equivalent of Popeye popping open a can of spinach. And they aren't shy about letting people know this.

I cannot even count the number of times I have heard someone warn someone else with the words, "You had better not get me mad!" Well, simply put, this is unwise and faulty thinking. What these people are actually saying is that if you continue to push their buttons, they will lose control and allow their emotions and anger to dictate their actions. It is music to the ears of the trained warrior when he hears his enemy say this, because at that time he knows his enemy is defeated.

Taunting an enemy to the point of losing control is an ancient battle tactic. It has been used throughout the centuries to defeat one's enemies. Losing your temper doesn't make you stronger or more dangerous, at least not more dangerous to your opponent. It merely demonstrates your lack of control. Once you lose control, you don't think rationally. In a physical confrontation, you must be able to think rationally. If you find that you have no choice but to fight, keep your temper in check.

75

The traditional forms must be practiced correctly; real combat is another matter.
Gichin Funakoshi

Practicing katas or forms is a regular part of most martial arts dojos. Many martial artists debate both the purpose and the usefulness of practicing katas. The fact is, kata practice is useful, if performed correctly. By correctly, I'm not just talking about making sure each move is right. I'm talking about your whole attitude. You should perform katas with intensity, as if you are fighting imaginary opponents. Visualize these enemies attacking you as you block and counter.

When practiced correctly, kata practice is useful in several ways. First, it helps you learn the principles behind your art. It is a good cardio workout for your body which strengthens both your stances and your techniques. Also, when you practice your kata over and over, it enables you to internalize your techniques, making them automatic. Finally, it allows you to practice going into mushin, the state of mind where you allow your body to perform without consciously having to think about your actions.

Taking all this into consideration, I do believe that kata practice is useful, but correct form is not what matters in real combat. What matters in real combat is using whatever works. If you are thinking about how you should punch or kick in a street fight you are finished. These techniques have to come automatically when you need them. Fighters who are skilled in street fighting enter into a state of mushin, whether they know it or not. They fight instinctively, and so should you. Think about this.

76

Treat every encounter as a fight to the finish.
The Eight Essentials for Novice Swordsmen

The human body is very fragile. Any physical encounter should be taken seriously, as there is always the chance of being injured when you find yourself in a combative situation. Even if you win, the old saying holds true; when two tigers fight, one will be killed and the other will be injured. Never underestimate your enemy or his ability to do bodily injury to you. Treat every violent confrontation as a possible life-or-death situation.

Treating every physical encounter as a fight to the finish ensures that you are in the right frame of mind for the fight. You must have your mind focused on the task at hand, which is to make sure you are safe, and to destroy your enemy's will to continue to be a threat to you or those around you. Don't allow overconfidence to slip into your mind. There are no small enemies. Overconfidence can lead to your demise. Every fight is a serious fight. If it isn't serious, you have no business fighting.

I'm not suggesting that by treating every physical threat as a fight to the finish, you should kill your opponent whenever you enter into a fight. This should be common sense. What I am saying is that you should enter that fight with the mindset that your enemy wants to kill you, and act accordingly in your self-defense applications. Never count on someone's mercy or self-control in this type of situation. You take control. Make sure that you are safe, not because your enemy is unwilling to really hurt you, but by ensuring that he is unable to hurt you.

77

When the world is at peace, a gentleman keeps his sword by his side.
Wu Tsu

We are very blessed to live in a time of peace and stability in our country. For the most part, our citizens live in a peaceful world, at least while they are close to home. It has been this way for years in our country, but if history has taught us anything, it is that this world is constantly changing. Countries rise and fall. Peace is disrupted by war. Governments are overthrown and replaced. Nothing stays the same for very long.

Change is the one thing that you can count on in this world. It doesn't pay to become complacent just because you are now living in peaceful times. The wise man will stay as prepared as possible, in order to meet the challenges of this changing world. He realizes that peace rarely lasts for long, and that when times change, they often change violently and without notice.

What Wu Tsu is trying to tell us in this quote above, is that during times of peace, the warrior should keep his weapons ready, by his side. Don't become lazy and allow your weapons, your martial arts skills, to become rusty. Stay prepared and keep your weapons in good shape. Remember, even in the sheath, the knife must be sharp. Take care to keep your skills sharp, even in times of peace. The skill which is not practiced deteriorates. It is part of the warrior's duty to keep his skills sharp and to practice his art and to be ready when he is called upon to use those skills.

78

One should have learning on the left and the martial arts on the right.
Hojo Nagauji

The warrior should not be some uneducated brute. There is a difference in someone who merely knows how to fight or who has a sufficient amount of shear strength, and someone who is a true warrior. Balance is an important part of the warrior lifestyle, and learning and education is part of that balance, especially in today's world. Without education, whether formal or otherwise obtained, the warrior is at a distinct disadvantage today.

Learning doesn't have to come from years of college experience. There are many forms of education and many ways to obtain a well-rounded education. Many times a college education doesn't equate to true education. If someone truly wants to educate themselves on a subject, it can be done from books and from the internet. The point is, no matter how you choose to go about it, you should make sure that you balance your life with learning, as well as martial arts, character training, meditation, etc.

Spend time learning about things that interest you. Become well read. Study the subjects which apply to the warrior lifestyle, as well as staying informed about worldly affairs. The key to education, as with most other things in this life, is balance. You should know something about finances, investments, business, etc. You should know how things work around your house. It is impossible to be self-reliant and self-sufficient without the proper knowledge. A well-rounded education will serve you well.

79

Warriors aren't born, and they aren't made... they create themselves through trial and error and by their ability to conquer their own frailties and faults.

Philip J. Messina

It takes a lot to live the warrior lifestyle. You will make mistakes and fall short at times as you work to perfect each area of your life. What is important is that you never quit working to improve yourself. Continually work to perfect your character. Hone your martial arts skills to a fine edge and then keep them sharp. Slow down and take time to keep your mind calm through meditation and study.

Confucius stated that he wasn't born with the knowledge that he had; he worked hard to obtain it. In the same way, no one is born with all the traits of warriorhood. They have to be developed over time, through trial and error and hard work. Living the life of the warrior is a decision that one makes. Once the decision is made to walk the path of the warrior, then the real work begins. Making the decision to live the life of the warrior is only the first step in a long process.

Victories begin to be won as you conquer your shortcomings and overcome your mistakes. Each time you resist the temptation to lower your standards or to slack off in your training, you add another notch in your belt. You are constantly creating your character as you live the warrior lifestyle. Men can be taught to fight, but they develop character through their own efforts. As Gichin Funakoshi stated, "The ultimate goal of karate is the perfection of character." This is also the ultimate goal of the warrior lifestyle.

80

You cannot step twice into the same river.
Heraclitus

Change is the one thing that you can count on in this life. It doesn't matter what the situation may be, it is sure to change over time. If you currently find yourself in bad times, take heart, the bad times will not last. Nothing stays stagnant, everything is in flux. You may not be able to recognize that things are changing, but be assured, change is taking place. True, things may not be changing as fast as you would like, but they are changing.

Yes, it is hard going through these changes, but "hard" is not impossible. What doesn't destroy you only makes you stronger. Don't let the changes which time brings about destroy you. Take them and use them to build your strength and character. Know that nothing stays the same. Bad times will not stand! There is a purpose for everything in this life. Find the purpose in the changes that you are going through.

There is never a time in this life for the warrior to be complacent. In bad times, you must work to improve your standing. In good times, you must strive to maintain your position. The warrior is always wary of the changes that inevitably come around as the winds of time silently weave threads of transformation through our lives.

Don't become complacent when times are good, and don't give in to despair when times are bad. No matter what changes time brings to you, deal with those changes like the noble warrior that you are. As Hemingway put it, "Grace under pressure." There is a purpose for everything in this life. Find the purpose in the changes that you are going through.

81

Do not show any intention.
Gichin Funakoshi

If you have ever watched any of the professional poker players playing in a Texas Hold'em tournament, you have seen the extent that they go to in order to hide their intentions. There is a reason for this. They do not want the other players to be able to "read" them. The players don't want there to be any sign of what they are thinking or what they are planning on doing. Confusion and deception are the tools of their trade. This is where the term "poker face" comes from.

Likewise, the warrior should keep his intentions hidden, especially in any confrontation. Trying to resolve confrontations without allowing them to become physical involves skill and a certain amount of deception. You are attempting to placate someone who in all probability deserves a good butt kicking. Your objective is to defeat him without him even knowing that he has been defeated. This is where deception comes into play.

To the other guy, you may seem weak. You may seem like you are trying to avoid a fight in order to save your own skin, but this is all a charade. You aren't afraid to fight, but rather you have decided to defeat your enemy without having to fight, which is a much more rewarding victory. Don't allow your intention to show. Defeat your enemy with your most powerful weapon – your mind.

82

Do not think dishonestly.
Miyamoto Musashi

I have already discussed how the warrior should be honest. Honesty and sincerity are both basic traits of the warrior lifestyle. The warrior should never be dishonest with others for personal gain or selfish reasons. This is just a basic tenet of honor and integrity and is something that men of virtue take for granted as being a fundamental part of the warrior lifestyle.

As important as it is for you to be honest in your dealings with others, it is even more so for you to be honest with yourself. Yes, you can be dishonest with yourself. You have to think honestly. By this, I mean that you have to see things as they truly are, not as you wish they were or as you want them to be. You must assess each specific thing as honestly as possible. There is no advantage for the warrior in thinking dishonestly, but there are many disadvantages to being dishonest with yourself.

People in general have a tendency to be dishonest with themselves on many occasions. They don't want something to be a certain way, so they refuse to believe that things are the way that they really are. For example, a man may lose $1,000 at the casino and feel awful about losing his money, so he may try to justify it by rationalizing that it was just entertainment and he would have spent the money anyway, so it was not like he actually "lost the money." This type of rationalizing the situation is thinking dishonestly. See things as they truly are and be honest with yourself. It is the way of the warrior.

83

Protecting yourself is self-defense.
Protecting others is warriorship.
Bohdi Sanders

Many people consider themselves to be warriors just because they have spent time training in a dojo and have learned how to fight. They feel that they can protect themselves against almost any attacker. Having developed their skills to the max, they walk around with the self-confidence of a lion, just waiting for some poor soul to make the mistake of harassing them in a bar or on the street. They feel without a shadow of a doubt that they can protect themselves, but does this really make them a warrior?

Protecting yourself is self-defense by the very definition of the term. Being a warrior means much more than being able to protect yourself. It means being willing and able to protect others as well as yourself. Warriors feel a sense of duty to protect those around them where the ordinary man only feels the need to protect himself and get out of Dodge. There is a big difference in the two.

The warrior is willing to put his well-being on the line for those he loves or for those under his protection. Many times, he puts their well being ahead of his own. He could easily defend himself and leave the danger behind, but he chooses the path of chivalry and warriorship. He knows there is a difference between self-defense and warriorship, and he also knows that the lifestyle that he has chosen demands that he put his warrior ideals over simple self-interest. Protecting yourself is self-defense; protecting others is warriorship.

84

It is truly regrettable that a person will treat a man who is valuable to him well, and a man who is worthless to him poorly.
Hojo Shigetoki

It is not honorable to treat people with respect only when you feel they are or could be valuable to you in some way. This has probably been a common practice ever since men began to socialize, and it is also a hypocritical practice. If you are treating someone in a respectful manner only because they could be useful to you at a later time, you are not being sincere, but rather being manipulative. Don't use or manipulate people in order to serve your own selfish purposes.

The warrior should treat everyone he meets with respect, whether he sees them as valuable to him or not. He treats people with respect because treating people with respect is part of the lifestyle which he has chosen. The warrior lifestyle is a lifestyle of honor, and it is honorable to treat everyone you meet with due respect. If you want to be respected, respect others. You should treat others as you would have them treat you. Treating someone with respect has nothing to do with whether or not they actually deserve respect.

Warriors may have to manipulate certain circumstances at times, but he still treats everyone he meets with respect, even those who do not deserve his respect. His actions are determined by his own code, and not how others live their lives. He treats others in a certain manner because that is the kind of man that he has decided to be, not because they do or do not deserve to be treated with respect or kindness. Respect is given out of a sense of honor.

85

Many are stubborn in pursuit of the path they have chosen, few in pursuit of the goal.
Friedrich Nietzsche

In whatever position you find yourself, first determine your objective. You have to know what your ultimate objective is. What is your purpose? When you are at a restaurant or pub with your family or friends, and some thug starts to get aggressive and rude, what is your ultimate objective in that situation? Is it to save face or to look good in front of your friends and family? Is it to look like the tough guy?

Absolutely not! Those are selfish goals and can actually interfere with what should be your real goal – to make sure that you and those around you are safe. This is your ultimate goal as a warrior. It is your duty to protect those around you, not to look like "Mr. Cool" or "Joe Tough Guy." Always keep your ultimate objective in mind when you have to deal with some thug in the street. This means that you have to remain calm and think rationally. Keep your emotions out of the equation.

The best way to make sure that everyone remains safe is to keep things from getting physical. Use your mind and your wit to defeat your opponent. Manipulate him without him ever knowing that he is being manipulated. If you have to swallow a little pride in order to accomplish your goal, do it. That is a small price to pay to keep those you love safe.

Always be nice until it is time to not be nice. Your intuition and your spirit will let you know when that time comes. This can't be accomplished if you allow your emotions to influence your decisions. Think rationally and accomplish your ultimate objective.

86

Perceive things that are not obvious.
Miyamoto Musashi

Anyone can see the obvious, well almost anyone. It seems more and more people are getting to the point that even the obvious is too complicated for them to discern. People who only look at the exterior of things are easily deceived. They are sheep, led to the slaughter by unscrupulous men. Dishonorable men present information to the public just as a fisherman presents a baited hook to a fish. The tempting bait is obvious; the razor sharp hook is hidden.

The warrior has to look beyond the obvious and perceive things which are hidden. Know that most people are presenting information to you either from their prejudiced point of view or with some hidden motive which you know nothing about. The wise man has to be able to see beyond the bait to discern whether or not there is a hidden trap just waiting to ensnare him.

Train yourself to see the angle when someone is presenting you with information. Today, more than ever, you have to watch out for scams and misleading information. Don't allow yourself to fall victim to someone else's cleverly baited trap. The warrior has to make sure that his decisions are made according to facts, not smoke and mirrors. Take the time to investigate things fully before giving your word concerning anything questionable. Never rush into something without looking behind the veil. Perceive what at first appears hidden in order to know what others don't want you to know.

87

Every action we take, everything we do, is either a victory or defeat in the struggle to become what we want to be.

Anne Byrhhe

This is a very strong statement for the warrior to consider. Every action, everything you think, everything you say, and everything you do, is either bringing you closer to your goals or further away from your goals, on your quest for warriorship. Every little thing matters. This is a very powerful thought.

Did your actions last night bring you closer to your goals or take you further away from your goals. I'm not talking about whether or not they were right or wrong, but only were they helpful or a hindrance. There is nothing wrong with going out to dinner, but if you go out and load up on unhealthy foods, along with excessive amounts of alcohol, your actions definitely did not bring you closer to your goals as a warrior.

Start looking at each action with this quote in mind, and ask yourself, "Is this action going to make me a better person, spiritually, mentally, or physically?" If the answer is no, then maybe you need to reconsider this action. It takes practice to slow down and think about your actions and the consequences that each of them will have on your goals. This is not an easy thing to do, but just as your martial arts skills are difficult at first and then become easier, so shall your struggle to become what you are trying to become, a man of excellence who has perfected his character.

88

We ought to do everything both cautiously and confidently at the same time.
Epictetus

The warrior should always be aware of his surroundings. This doesn't mean that he is constantly walking around, nervously looking for trouble, but that he is aware of what is going on around him. He observes the people he encounters and pays attention to their behavior. When dealing with others, he reads between the lines and is cautious about believing what he sees. It is in his nature to be cautious because he knows the nature of most men.

At the same time, he acts with confidence. His cautious nature allows him to go through life with confidence. He is aware of what is going on around him. He has done his homework and therefore is a confident player in the game. Being cautious is not being fearful or cowardly; it is being safe and prepared. Only when you feel prepared are you able to feel confident in different situations.

Your martial arts training gives you confidence in dealing with violent situations, but you still have to enter into any physical confrontation with extreme caution. This is a good example of doing something with both caution and confidence at the same time. You have confidence that you can defeat your attacker, but you are still cautious. Being overconfident and careless can cost you your life. No matter how sharp you believe your skills to be, always enter every confrontation with the utmost caution.

89

One bad example destroys more than twenty good.
Hungarian Proverb

We have all seen in the news, the lifelong politician who suddenly falls from grace because of a poor choice or ridiculous indiscretion. It happens over and over again. The news media loves it when someone in power makes a bad mistake. They then go in and exploit his mistake for their ratings. When this happens, no one ever remembers any of the good things this man has accomplished. All the attention is on the one bad choice.

The politician's one bad example has destroyed what may have been years of dedicated service to his country. His good deeds are no longer news worthy. His character is now in question and many times is destroyed, all by one single action. The action of a single minute can destroy the reputation that it took a lifetime to build. Although hypocrites and crooked men should be brought to light, it is still a sad moment when any man destroys his character and reputation with unwise choices.

The warrior should keep this in mind. No matter how many good deeds you accomplish or how far you have come in the perfection of your character, it can all be trashed by one bad decision or one moment's loss of control. As a man of honor and integrity, your reputation should be above reproach. Don't give your enemies what they need to take you down by making poor decisions. Always remember that it only takes one bad decision to destroy the fruits of many good decisions. Be careful.

90

Never do anything against conscience even if the state demands it.
Einstein

As a warrior, your own conscience should be so highly developed that it becomes the ultimate factor in determining your every action. This will not happen automatically. It takes study, practice, and correcting the many mistakes that you will make along the way, but once you have accomplished the task of perfecting your character, your conscience will be your most reliable guide. When you get to this place in your training, all you have to be concerned about is living by the dictates of your conscience.

It is vital that you don't do anything that goes against your conscience. This is equivalent to breaking your code of ethics. If you feel inside that an action is not the correct action to take, then don't take it. Learn to trust your instinct or your intuition. Once you have developed your conscience through time and patience, it will not steer you wrong, but you must trust it enough to act on what you feel.

This also takes a lot of practice, as well as courage. It takes courage to go against the majority just because you don't feel right on the inside about the issue at hand. Start listening to your intuition in small matters. Slow down, quiet your mind, and listen to your intuition. Then follow what you feel. Develop this skill in small, non-essential matters, and it will serve you well when more critical situations suddenly appear in your life. The warrior lifestyle has many components, and each must be developed through training and discipline. Listen to your conscience.

91

Highly evolved people have
their own conscience as pure law.
Lao Tzu

As a warrior, you have to consider what is right in all your actions. Legal does not necessarily equal right, and illegal does not necessarily equal wrong. There may be times when the warrior has to decide between what is right and what is legal. Yes, sometimes the warrior has to do things which may be against the law. Conversely, there are many things which are considered legal according to our laws, which the warrior will consider dishonorable according to the code by which he lives.

This may sound strange to many of you, but it is reality for the warrior. An example that many people can relate to would be the issue of abortion. Abortion is legal in this country, but there are millions of Christians in our country who would not consider abortion an ethical option. It goes against their principles. In the same way, there are many things which are legal which go against the principles which the warrior lives by.

Einstein said that one should "Never do anything against conscience even if the state demands it." This describes the warrior perfectly. He never goes against his code of honor. His honor is his law. The warrior must do things which are illegal at times in order to hold fast to his integrity and honor. The warrior doesn't need laws to keep him in line. His own sense of right and wrong, and his sense of honor and integrity keep a tighter rein on his actions than any outside law. Even if there were no laws at all, the warrior would still do the right thing.

92

It is not the oath that makes us believe the man, but the man the oath.
Aeschylus

It seems that not many people keep their word in today's society. People will lie straight to your face in order to get what they want, and they will not even feel bad afterwards. Today, when someone gives you a promise, unless you are dealing with a man of honor, that promise is virtually meaningless. It is not the promise or the "oath" that gives us a sense of security, but rather it is the honor of the man who gives you his word.

With most people, it is wise to get any agreement in writing, and even then, have that written contract checked for loopholes which will give dishonorable people a way to not live up to their promises. Their word is almost worthless. This in turn gives us insight into their character. If their word is worthless, so is their character. Never trust the word of a man of low character. To do so is not only unwise, but it is simply foolishness.

The warrior is a man of character, honor and integrity. He is a man of his word. His reputation precedes him and people know that when he gives his word, they can rely on him to back it up with his actions. You don't have to worry about a man of honor not keeping his word. To do so would be against his standards. We know that we can believe the oath because we know that we can depend on his honor. This is one of many traits which sets the true warrior apart from the rest of society. Your word should be your bond; your word should be your honor.

93

The superior man is watchful over himself even when alone.
Chung Yung

Although the number of people who do not observe manners in public is drastically increasing, the vast majority of people seem to behave well when they are away from home. They are watchful over their behavior and manners when they are out on the town, but at home or alone, they tend to live differently. This should not be so for the warrior. The warrior should be aware of his actions at all times, whether alone or in public.

Chung Yung reiterates the teaching of Confucius and tells us that the superior man, the warrior, is watchful over himself at all times, even when he is alone. This doesn't mean that the warrior doesn't relax at home or that he is constantly uptight. It means that he is careful to do what is right, whether he is out in public, around his family, or home alone where no one else sees his actions. The point to this teaching is that the warrior should live according to his standards at all times.

Time, place and company do not affect the warrior's dedication to his code of honor. He remains true to his code regardless of where he is or who is with him. Even alone he is careful to do what is right. He is not acting for the benefit of others. The opinions of others are not what concern him. The warrior is concerned with his duty and doing the right thing. His conscience guides him and he knows that he must answer only to himself, but to the man of honor, that is the highest authority, besides God. Be a superior man and keep a tight rein on yourself at all times.

94

The word friend is common, the fact is rare.
Phaedrus

An acquaintance is simply someone who you know or who you are on friendly terms with, whereas as the term friend has a much deeper meaning. To me a true friend is a very rare person to find today. A friend is someone who will stand by you through thick and thin. When the chips are down, your friend is there with you. When the wolf is at your door, your friend is standing inside the door with you, ready to put his life on the line, side by side with you. He will stand by you, right or wrong. When you win the lottery, your friend is sincerely happy for you, just as if he had won it himself. Are you getting the picture?

I consider a friend to be much more than an acquaintance. In truth, you are lucky to have one true friend in your life. If you have more than one, you are truly blessed. Realize this and don't make the mistake of thinking of your acquaintances as your true friends. This is a common mistake that people make, and when their back is against the wall, they are shocked to find that they really don't have friends, but only acquaintances that can disappear like a dove in a magic show.

Strive to make sure that your true friends are men of character, honor, and integrity. Warriors are the best of friends. Because they live by a strict code of ethics; they refuse to let their friends down in their time of need. This would go against their nature and their code. When you have developed a true friendship with a warrior, you have a trusted friend for life.

95

The superior man does not give up good conduct because the inferior man rails against him.
Hsun-Tzu

The warrior is a man of principle. He doesn't set his principles aside when they seem inconvenient. Today many people do just that. They use the actions of others to justify their own bad behavior. Statements such as, "Well I wouldn't have done that if he hadn't shoved me, cursed me, been rude to me, etc." are commonly heard to justify bad behavior. The warrior should not allow the behavior of others to affect his own behavior, at least not as far as doing things that are against his principles.

Of course, as a warrior, there may be times when the actions of others may cause you to have to take action, but this is different than allowing someone else's actions to affect how you respond as far as your principles are concerned. The warrior must respond, not react. Even if you have to take physical action in a specific situation, you can still do so without lowering your principles. The true man of principle can't set his principles aside. They are a part of him, a part of his spirit and who he truly is as a human being.

Someone else being what they are, whether it is an obnoxious thug, a criminal, or whatever, should not cause you to forget the fact that you are a man of principle. Don't allow the actions of others to cause you to compromise your principles. This is an easy trap to walk into, and a flimsy excuse for poor behavior. The warrior never forgets what he is and never sets aside his principles. Think rationally and remember who you are and what you are.

96

The path of the warrior is a noble path and a lifelong quest for excellence.
Bohdi Sanders

If you have chosen the path of the warrior as your lifestyle, you have chosen the road less traveled. The warrior lifestyle consists of a life of honor, integrity, hard work, and service to others. It is a noble path and one which only the best of men chose to walk. It is a quest for excellence in all areas of one's life. But what is the ultimate goal of the warrior lifestyle?

You probably know that the ultimate goal of Christianity is to go to Heaven. The ultimate goal of Buddhism is to reach Nirvana. The ultimate goal for a boxer is to be the world champion. But is there an ultimate goal when it comes to the warrior lifestyle? Yes and no. The warrior lifestyle does not consist of a quest where you reach your goal and then relax, knowing that you have accomplished what you set out to accomplish, but there is an actual goal involved which the warrior seeks endlessly to achieve.

That goal is the perfection of one's character. The perfection of one's character is an ongoing process. You may think that you have reached a point of perfection one day, only to find that you have lost it in a single second the next by making a bad choice. Therefore, this is not a finite goal like winning the championship belt in boxing. This is a never-ending quest to improve yourself. The warrior realizes that his goal is a lifelong quest and a noble path which is only rarely taken. It is not the easiest path to take, but it is the most rewarding. Walk the noble path – the path of the warrior.

97

It is no easy thing for a principle to become a man's own unless each day he maintains it and works it out in his life.
Epictetus

Developing your character takes work. It takes patience, dedication and perseverance. It is not an easy thing to do, at least not at first. There will constantly be temptations to step away from your principles. This is why the perfection of your character is a never-ending process. The opportunities to slide backwards are never-ending; therefore the opportunities for new victories over yourself are endless.

Each day you have to work at maintaining your character. You have to work at developing your principles. It will become easier and easier as your principles become second nature to you, but you will still have temptations to compromise those principles, even once you have made them your own. Developing your character and living by a set of principles is not a goal, but an ongoing process. It takes work and discipline to resist the many temptations to compromise your standards.

You can liken this to the wise fish who never takes the bait. This fish has learned the strategies of the fishermen. He recognizes all the various baits and lures that he has been tempted with over the years. Yet no matter how many times he resists the newest temptation that the fishermen cast into his pond, the next day he can be assured that he will be presented with another one. It only takes one bad decision for the wise old fish to end up in the frying pan. Think about this.

98

Let them know a real man, who lives as he was meant to live.
Marcus Aurelius

The vast majority of people think that the term "man" and the term "male" are synonymous, but the sages throughout the ages have always disagreed with this. Many of the great sages taught that there is a difference in being a male and a true man. Confucius made this distinction with the terms "superior man" and "inferior man." Marcus Aurelius made this distinction by referring to a man of honor and integrity as a "real man."

In today's society, the mere mention of the "real" man is met with sneers and ridicule, usually followed by rude and crude comments. Most people can't wrap their minds around the concept that you earn the right to be called a man. Just because you are born a male doesn't necessarily mean you are a man. The term "man" as used here, could be synonymous with the term "true human being." When looked at in this way, there is a big difference between being a male and being a man.

This distinction is really only recognized by those whose philosophy leans towards that which is found in the warrior lifestyle. Warriors know that there is a difference in the way a real man lives as compared to the inferior man. Real men live a life of character, honor and integrity. They take care of their family and filial duties. They serve and protect those around them. They live by a strict code of standards. In short, they are warriors. Let the world know a real man; don't sell yourself short. Live the warrior lifestyle.

99

Knowing is not enough, we must apply. Willing is not enough, we must do.
Goethe

You may have the knowledge concerning what it takes to live the warrior lifestyle, and you may think that you are willing to make the sacrifices that it takes to follow through with that lifestyle, but that is not enough. It is not enough to have the knowledge about something without putting that knowledge to use. It is not enough to be willing to do something; you must actually take action.

Too many people read book after book, gaining a little knowledge on this and a little knowledge on that, without ever putting anything that they learn to use. We have more information available to us today than at any time in human history, yet ignorance is still rampant. It does you no good to learn something if that knowledge is not going to be put to use in some constructive way.

The warrior should have knowledge about various things, but he should also make use of that knowledge. He must apply what he knows to the warrior lifestyle. Knowledge without action is like having money without ever spending it. It does you no good. You continue to earn money so that you can use that money to provide for yourself and your family. Likewise, you should continue to increase your knowledge so you can use that knowledge to better yourself and your life. Don't hoard knowledge, apply it.

100

Do nothing to make you lose respect for yourself.
Baltasar Gracian

The respect that you have for yourself can't be taken away from you by anyone else. You are the only person who controls the level of respect that you do or don't have for yourself. Other people can try to hurt you, embarrass you, humiliate you, etc., but they can't control your own feelings toward yourself. You control your self-respect just as you determine your own honor.

So if others can do nothing to cause you to lose your self-respect, how do you lose respect for yourself? Obviously it can be lost or Gracian would not have admonished us to be careful about losing self-respect. The answer is that you lose self-respect when you lower your standards or do not live up to your own code of conduct that you have set for yourself. The warrior knows inside his spirit if he is living up to his code of honor or not. Only he can determine that.

When he knows inside that he is not living up to his own standards, he starts to lose a bit of his self-respect. If he refused to help someone because of fear, that action would eat away at him until he made it right. This is because of the strict standards which he sets for himself. He knows that he must do what is right in order to feel at peace with his own actions. Anything less and his conscience will not let him be at peace. Warriors esteem their honor too highly to allow themselves to lose self-respect because of weakness or laziness. When you live up to your code of honor you never lose self-respect

101

Though the wind blows,
the mountain does not move.
Japanese Proverb

The warrior has to be able to stand up against the majority without allowing them to sway what he knows is right. No matter how vocally or violently people stand up against you, when you know that you are right, do not be persuaded to give in. Never turn your back on what is just, no matter how hard the wind blows against you. The just man is his own law and should not resemble a politician who changes his standards according to which side is in the majority.

Emerson wrote that in order to be an individual, a man must be willing to stand alone, against all others if necessary. This is a good description of the warrior. He must have the courage to stand for what is right no matter what. It doesn't matter if all other men hold the opposite point of view. It doesn't matter if no one will stand by his side. He still stands for what he knows is right.

The warrior's code of honor is more important to him than the opinions of others. So much so that he is able to withstand any attempts that others may make to sway his opinions. In order to have this much conviction in your beliefs, you have to be totally convinced that you are right. This means that you have to spend time in deep thought and meditation, and that you have to actually know what you believe and why. The warrior is truly the mountain that the winds of opinion cannot move.

102

The superior man is governed by decorum; the inferior man is ruled by law.
Confucius

Do you need laws in order to persuade you to do the right thing? Well, if you are a true warrior you don't. Confucius taught that laws were made to keep the "inferior man" in check. The superior man, the warrior, is not governed by laws, but rather is governed by his own sense of right and wrong, and his dignity. The warrior doesn't rely on politicians to debate and tell him what he should and should not do. The laws passed by these people have very little effect on the life of the warrior, other than following the basic rules of the society in which he lives.

Men of character and honor do not need other men to tell them what is right and what is wrong. They do not require laws to keep them from committing acts which are dishonorable or unscrupulous. Warriors live by a higher law than the law of the land. These superior men live by their code of honor, and this code demands that they hold themselves to a higher standard.

Do you need laws in order to do what you should? Would you lower your standards concerning stealing, committing fraud, etc. if suddenly there were no more laws against such actions? The man of honor would live the same life of integrity even if all laws were abolished because he is ruled by decorum and not the opinions of other men. Laws are nothing more than rules of conduct developed by a group of men and enforced by other men. The man of honor is, in effect, his own law. He develops his own code of conduct, and he lives by that code without fail.

103

A just man. He stands on the side of right with such conviction, that neither the passion of the mob, nor the violence of a despot can make him overstep the bounds of reason.
Baltasar Gracian

Are you a just man? Do you stand for what is right and do so with so much conviction that no man can persuade you to lower your standards? Do you have the courage to maintain your own convictions concerning justice, even if everyone else disagrees with you, or if others are threatening violence if you refuse to change? These are questions which the warrior must ask himself.

Baltasar Gracian was a wise man. He also taught that the majority is almost always in the wrong, therefore if you want to stand for what is right, you will most likely have to be willing to stand against the majority. You have to have the backbone to go against the flow, but at the same time, you should do so in an intelligent way. There is a right way and a wrong way to do everything.

Maintain your standards no matter what obstacles are placed in your path, but realize that there are many ways to overcome these obstacles. It is not always wise to fight. Sometimes it is much wiser to peacefully step around an obstacle rather than destroying the obstacle which is blocking your path. Always think about what your ultimate objective is and then work to achieve your objective in the most efficient way possible.

Are you a just man? Do you have enough conviction concerning what is right, in order to stand against the tide of public opinion? This is something that has to be developed in the life of the warrior.

104

Warriors should never be thoughtless or absentminded but handle all things with forethought.
Shiba Yoshimasa

Think before you act. This is a simple philosophy, yet it seems, one that is rarely used in today's society. Many people just act without giving their actions any thought, and then deal with whatever consequences come about from their thoughtless actions. How much better would it be for everyone involved if people would give forethought to their actions before they actually made a move?

The way many people act is completely backwards to the way in which they should act. They act and then think about the consequences, when they should think about the consequences first, then make a decision about which action they should take. This is the way that the warrior should go about things. Don't be thoughtless or absentminded. Give thought to your actions before you act.

Always think things through to the best of your abilities. Keep your mind engaged, no matter how important or how trivial the matter at hand may be. Remember that every action carries with it a consequence, and what may seem trivial could turn into something much more important if the wrong decision is made. Thoughtless actions can take on a life of their own and cause you problems that you never imagined, and which could have completely been avoided with a little forethought. THINK!

105

What I must do is all that concerns me, not what the people think.
Emerson

Your job as a warrior is to focus on what you should do and how you should act. You do what you know is right and what should be done. If you do this, you have done your part; you have done your duty as a warrior. Don't be upset or disturbed if things don't turn out exactly as you wanted or expected. All you can do is act on what you know to be right, and do the best that you can do in the present moment.

Don't worry about what someone else does or does not do. You are not responsible for their actions. Don't let your mind be unsettled by the way things turn out after you have done your best. Be rational. If things do not turn out the way that you had hoped, all you can do is decide what your next step should be and once again, act in the moment. You only have control over certain things. Control what you can, and be at peace with the things which you can't change.

Being distressed about the way things are will not change anything and is wasted time and energy. Don't spend time in worry or regret. Decide what the right course of action is for every point in time, and then follow through and act. Marcus Aurelius taught this very same wisdom hundreds of years before Emerson. He stated, "I do what is mine to do; the rest doesn't disturb me." This is good advice for the warrior. Instead of being disturbed over the things which you can't change, focus on those that you can.

106

The superior man enacts equity, and justice is the foundation of all his deeds.
Confucius

Confucius spoke often of the "superior man" in his teachings. If we look at all of the qualities that Confucius attributes to the "superior man" we could easily replace the words "superior man" with the word "warrior." In fact the warrior is a superior man in every sense of the word. To the warrior, equity and justice is the foundation of all his deeds. His character is built on this foundation.

One of the definitions of equity is justice tempered by ethics. Justice tempered by ethics describes the lifestyle of the warrior perfectly. The warrior's sense of right and wrong, his sense of ethics, is definitely the foundation of his actions. He spends many hours meditating on right and wrong and developing his code of ethics, to ensure that he lives a life of honor. He takes great pains to ensure that his actions are just.

Another definition of both equity and justice is that of fairness or reasonableness in the way people are treated or the way decisions are made. These traits are part of the warrior lifestyle which guides the warrior in his dealings with others. He uses reason and fairness as his guide in all his relationships with others. His honor does not allow him to lie, cheat or steal when dealing with others in business or in personal affairs. Make sure that equity and justice are the foundation to all of your deeds, and you will be well on your way to living the warrior lifestyle.

107

For when moral value is considered, the concern is not the actions, which are seen, but rather with their inner principles, which are not seen.
Kant

Can the right action be wrong? At first this may seem like a very simple question with a simple answer, but is it really? When you stop to think about this question, it becomes a little more involved. The answer depends on whether you are judging only the action itself or the moral intentions behind the action. According to Kant, the true test of whether an action is right or wrong lies not in the action itself, but in the principles behind the action.

This is also what the warrior should be concerned with when it comes to his actions. The warrior can do the right thing, but if he does it for the wrong reason or with evil intentions, is he really following his code of honor? I don't think so. The intentions or the "inner principles" behind the warrior's actions are very important. This is why many times it is impossible for someone else to truly judge another's actions as right or wrong.

Only the warrior knows if his intentions are just and honorable, and even if they are, he still has to make sure that his actions are right. You can have honorable intentions and still make the wrong choice as far as your actions go. For example, you could want to help the poor, but robbing a bank would be the wrong way to accomplish this goal. On the other hand, you can do what others may perceive as the right thing, but have less than honorable intentions, which can spoil the true integrity of your actions. Both your intentions and your actions have to be right. Think about this.

108

We are all ready to be savage in some cause. The difference between a good man and a bad one is the choice of the cause.
William James

Although many today profess to live by the mantra that there is never any excuse for violence, they will turn to violence when their back is against the wall. If some psychopath is about to murder their child or spouse, almost everyone would use violence to stop him from succeeding. The person being attacked by another with the intent to take his or her life will fight back, with only the rarest exceptions.

Every human being is capable of violence. We are all capable of turning into a savage depending on the situation at hand. Warriors know this and train for the time when they are forced by circumstances beyond their control to use their martial arts skills on another human being. They know that the mantra of "there is never any excuse for violence" is completely bogus, as are most absolute statements.

So is all violence bad? What makes one violent act any different than another? The answer is the cause for which you are fighting. There is a tremendous difference between savagely beating someone in order to take his wallet, and savagely beating someone to a pulp in order to insure the safety of your wife and children. The end result of the action upon another man is the same, but the principle behind the act is totally different. Once again, right and wrong have to do with the intentions behind the action more so than the action itself.

109

He who plants a forest in the morning cannot expect to saw planks the same evening.
Chinese Proverb

The warrior lifestyle takes time to perfect. It takes time to develop your character, to learn to automatically live by your code of honor, to serve and protect others when you would rather be minding your own business, and to develop the overall discipline that this lifestyle requires. All of these things do not come naturally; you have to work for them, and this takes time. Developing any worthwhile skill is a process, and developing your character is no different.

Voltaire taught that perfection is attained by slow degrees; she requires the hand of time. It doesn't matter what you are trying to perfect; nothing goes from the foundation to flawlessness over night. It takes time for a seed to grow into a full grown plant. It takes time for a baby to grow into a man. And it will take time for you to develop all of the skills and character traits that are a part of warriorhood. Knowing this, you must be patient with yourself when you miss your mark at times.

One of the main ingredients in success is determination. You must be determined not to give up. Don't quit! If you find that you have made a wrong move, and you will, don't throw in the towel and think that you can never measure up to the true warrior. Everyone makes mistakes. This is just part of the learning process of the warrior lifestyle. You will make mistakes. Learn from those mistakes and do better next time. You are never defeated until you declare defeat.

110

No weapon is sharper than the mind; even the finest sword is inferior.
The Masters of Huainan

No matter how much weapons training or martial arts training you have had, your best and most reliable weapon is your mind. That's right, your mind is your first weapon of self-defense, and just like any other weapon, you have to practice using it in order to be proficient with it when you need it. You have to train your mind concerning how to respond to certain situations, just as you have to train your body through strength training and martial arts training.

Once you have trained your mind to remain calm, no matter what condition you may find yourself in, you have taken a huge step in the preparation of your mental arsenal. You must learn to stay calm in the storm. A calm mind is a mind that can think rationally. It is sharp and focused. Stress, anxiety and panic all hinder the mind's ability to function properly and thus renders your most important weapon useless or at least not functioning at its peak.

There are several techniques that the warrior can use to train his mind to remain calm. Realistic martial arts training is a good way to accomplish this, as is meditation. Your martial arts training should be as realistic as possible. You have to learn how to control your mind under stressful situations such as when someone is in your face yelling and threatening you. This type of training technique enables you to feel what it is like to respond to a real threat. Keep your most useful weapon sharp and ready.

111

One should practice steadfast and indiscriminative virtue without demanding others to do the same in return.
Lao Tzu

Be independent! The warrior should do what he knows is right, regardless of what anyone else does or does not do. As Lao Tzu tells us in the *Tao Te Ching*, you should practice virtue, steadfastly and indiscriminately, independent of what others do. Your goal is to perfect your character, not to treat others as they treat you, as they appear to deserve, or as you would many times like to. You are not responsible for their actions or lack of action. You are not responsible for their character; you are responsible for your character.

Don't allow the rude, dishonorable acts of others to disrupt your progress. Be above their petty behavior. Keep your eye on your goal, and see their feeble character as nothing more than another challenge that you must face in your struggle to become the warrior that you want to be. They will reap the fruits of their actions, just as you will reap the fruits of your actions. If anything, you should feel sorry for them.

Focus on perfecting your own life and don't demand virtue from others. Knowing that true virtue is for the few, it should be no surprise to you when others demonstrate a lack of virtue. The warrior lifestyle is not for everyone. It is for the select few who dare to live with discipline and honor. Confucius would say it is for the superior man. It is silly to expect the inferior man to exhibit the same character traits as the superior man. Think about this.

112

Few man have virtue enough to withstand the highest bidder.
George Washington

Do you have the character to withstand the highest bidder? If you want to be a true warrior who walks the path of the warrior, the answer has to be yes. The warrior has to have the intestinal fortitude to put what is right above what is profitable when the two are at odds with each other. When you know that something is right and you allow someone to bribe you into overlooking the right action, you have lowered your standards.

This action will eat away at your soul if you are a warrior at heart. There are consequences to every action, even if those consequences aren't seen by the physical eye. The warrior is guided by his own conscience. He adheres to his code of honor, not because someone is forcing him to or because he is afraid of negative consequences, but because he has set a higher standard for himself – the standard of a true warrior. He answers to himself and himself alone.

For this reason, even if no one else on this planet ever found out about his selling out to the highest bidder, he would still never escape the fact that he knows about his compromise. His punishment is not physical, but rather a mental torment that comes from knowing that he lowered his standards. He put his honor on the shelf in return for a little monetary reward. This is a hard reality for the warrior to live with day in and day out. Don't sell out. Have the courage to walk the path of the warrior. Warrior honor is too valuable to sell to the highest bidder.

113

A truly virtuous person cannot be indifferent to the troubled world in which he lives.
Lao Tzu

Many people think that the truly enlightened person is the person who lives life as a monk, spending his time in isolation and meditation. Although there is a time and a place for retreating into solitude and spending time in meditation, the truly virtuous person, the warrior, will not be completely satisfied by this lifestyle. The warrior is dedicated to justice and righting wrongs; he cannot be satisfied hiding from the world's troubles.

People who are indifferent to the world's troubles are in reality being selfish. Sure, it is nice living a peaceful relaxed life, hidden away from the troubles and dangers of the world, but how is this helping anyone else? How is such a life being of service to those who desperately need help? Is living the life of a monk truly virtuous when looked at from this point of view? Not according to Lao Tzu's writings in the *Tao Te Ching*.

Lao Tzu taught that a truly virtuous person cannot be indifferent to the troubles of others or the world around him. His virtue requires that he try to help others as much as possible. Service to others is a part of a virtuous life, and it is a vital part of warriorhood. Don't be a selfish warrior, only thinking of yourself and your own goals. A major part of your training is to enable you to protect others. Make part of your aspirations to serve and protect others, and to improve their lives whenever you can.

114

The wise man never trusts in appearances.
Confucius

Appearances can be deceiving. This is just a fact of life. Confucius taught that the wise man should never trust in appearances. Instead of trusting in the cleverly scripted facade that most people present to you, try to look deeper. Look at the other person's objectives. What does he want from you? Is he presenting things the way that they actually are, or is he putting a specific spin on the matter at hand in order to influence your thought processes?

Most everyone makes an attempt to put their best foot forward when they are in public. You are not really seeing the "real person" in many cases. You are simply seeing the scripted person who is showing you the specific traits that they want you to think that they possess. Your job is to get beyond the act and find out who the real person is behind the nice clothes, good manners and careful speech. Remember that not everyone is up front and sincere, and not everyone is being honest.

This is not to say that everyone is disingenuous and that there are not those people who are sincere, but you have to determine who is sincere and who is not sincere. The same principle applies to every interaction with other individuals. Caveat emptor is Latin for let the buyer beware, and this is good advice whether you are buying a used car or someone's version of specific events. Beware that the wool is not pulled over your eyes. Hear both sides. Read between the lines. Do your homework, or as the Russian proverb states, "Trust but verify."

115

The wise pursue understanding;
fools follow the reports of others.
Tibetan Proverb

It seems it is getting harder and harder today to find an unbiased source for news. No matter which television station you watch, radio show you listen to, or news page on the internet that you read, it seems that they all have an agenda. It is foolish to blindly follow the reports of others, especially when those sources have hidden agendas which you are not privy to. With this in mind, you may ask, "What is a person to do if he wants to understand world events?"

That is a hard question to answer. The best you can do, if you do not have personal knowledge or have trustworthy friends with personal knowledge of what is going on, is to get your information from several different sources. This is akin to hearing both sides of the story. If you hear only one side, you will find that you are in the dark, as far as your understanding goes. Don't take things for the truth just because they are on television or because they are in writing.

Facts and statistics can be slanted to demonstrate whatever someone wants them to illustrate. Many people are experts when it comes to twisting the truth to fit their own personal agenda. Don't take what they say as gospel. No matter what the topic may be, strive to achieve an understanding of the issue. Trusting in the reports of others can prove dangerous and misleading. The warrior has to depend on the truth, not the spin.

116

Wise men do not argue with idiots.
Japanese Proverb

In the same way that one would not expect a first grade student to understand physics or chemistry, you should not expect idiots to comprehend the way of the warrior. They have no more capacity to understand the complexities of honor or the benefits of virtue than a dog has to program your DVD player. These concepts are totally foreign to them. They just don't understand the warrior lifestyle, and therefore should not be expected to carry on an intelligent conversation on the subject.

Oh, they will talk about the subject at length. They will talk as if they are the experts, not only on the subject of the warrior, but on virtually any other subject that may be brought up in the conversation. As the old saying goes, a fool talks because he has to say something; a wise man because he has something to say. There is a big difference between the two. Just as you could never explain to a summer insect the concept of snow, you will never be able to win an argument with people who do not think rationally.

It is wiser to just avoid the argument to start with and let them think what they will. Why should you care what they think? Their opinion, no matter how ridiculous, doesn't affect you. Don't waste your time arguing with these people. In fact, it is even wiser still, to not socialize with idiots. Call me "idiot intolerant," I have been called that before, but I had rather spend my time with men of character and honor. Your time on this earth is short, use it wisely.

117

It is the task of a good man to help those in misfortune.
Sophocles

When I was growing up I witnessed, time and time again, my grandfather helping those less fortunate who were in need of a helping hand. People would come to my grandfather's house and ask him for money, and every single time, without fail, he would loan or give them money. Hardly ever did anyone pay back the money that my grandfather had loaned them, but this never seemed to bother him.

One day, I saw a guy, which I personally knew to be dishonest and of low character, come to the door and ask for money, and as usual my grandfather gave this man money. After this man left with money in hand, I asked my grandfather why he had given this man money when he knew as well as I that this man would never repay him. He just told me that the man needed help, but that answer didn't satisfy me. I responded, but you know he is lying; he will never pay you back.

Then my grandfather said, "Well, it really wasn't a loan. I tell people that it is a loan so they don't feel uncomfortable about taking the money, but I am just giving the money to them to help them out. You see we have plenty. We have been greatly blessed and it is our duty to help those who are less fortunate than we are." Later in life, even after my family fell on hard times financially, my grandfather never quit helping others. He continued to help others financially, even when he didn't have the finances to do so. This is a characteristic of a good man.

118

He is the best man who, when making his plans, fears and reflects on everything that can happen to him, but in the moment of action is bold.
Herodotus

Some people have a false idea about who the warrior is as a person. They think that he is this brute who has no fear of death, or that he doesn't think before he acts, but rather acts out of pure adrenaline, not considering that he may be killed. This is not an accurate picture of the warrior. The warrior knows better than most, how fragile the human body is and how easily it can be destroyed. He has intricate knowledge about what can and does happen in physical encounters.

He knows the risks that he takes when he steps up to help someone who is being attacked by a mugger. He fully realizes what could happen if things go wrong. Warriors understand how much they have to lose and the consequences that certain situations could have on them and their family. They aren't born with some superior form of courage that makes them immune to fear. They develop their courage to the point that they are able to overcome their fear and do what must be done.

The warrior has the same human emotions as everyone else, but elects to control those emotions instead of being controlled by them. He realizes all of these things, but in the moment that someone needs his protection, he rises above all of these thoughts and emotions, and takes bold action. Warriors don't wait for someone else to take care of things because of their fear; they step up when they are needed. Herodotus said that this is a trait of the best men, and he is right, the true warrior is the best man.

119

He has honor if he holds himself to an ideal of conduct though it is inconvenient, unprofitable, or dangerous to do so.

Walter Lippmann

Sometimes it is tough living the warrior lifestyle. At times, the warrior has to make some hard decisions. What is right has to come before what is profitable, convenient, fun, or safe. The warrior walks by a stricter code of ethics than most people. While the average man bases his decisions on his own personal desires, the warrior looks at the bigger picture.

Warriors know that, in order to walk the road of honor, they must sometimes sacrifice other, easier roads. They realize that the easy path, although it is the path taken by most people, does not lead to the same peak as that of the steep path. Not all paths lead to the top of the mountain; some just meander around the base and never dare go where there is risk or danger. The warrior prefers to take the high road with all of its challenges, dangers and ultimately, its rewards.

The average man can't grasp why anyone would take the hard road instead of the easy road. Lesser men do not understand what honor really is, although he will claim to be an honorable man. To him, making a choice for himself that may be inconvenient, unprofitable, or dangerous is just plain not smart. He can't comprehend the mind of the warrior. Take the path that leads to the pinnacle of life. Don't settle for anything less than the best that you can be.

120

To avoid action when justice is at stake demonstrates a lack of courage.
Gichin Funakoshi

This is a strong statement from Master Funakoshi concerning courage and lack of courage, and should convict the heart of every warrior. You can't be a part of injustice. Justice is always on the mind of the warrior. When you are involved and you know something is not right, you have to take action. This is not to say that you have to jump in immediately and act rashly. There are many different kinds of action.

You should always consider your options and think rationally before you act. Not every act of injustice requires that you blatantly attack those involved. Of course, there can be times when you have to immediately intervene, but at other times it may be best to step back and plan what should be done to put things right. What Master Funakoshi is saying is that you shouldn't just turn your back and forget about the injustice.

You have to be willing to get involved and that always takes courage. Joseph Pulitzer said you should never tolerate injustice and corruption… never be afraid to attack wrong. This is essentially the same thing that Gichin Funakoshi was saying. The warrior has to stand for justice. It is part of his duty to help those who are in the right and cannot help themselves. The characters that we admire in movies and novels are the people who stand against injustice and try to set things right, yet it seems so few people actually have the courage to do this in their life. Have the courage to fight for justice when justice is at stake.

121

What lies in our power to do, it lies in our power not to do.
Aristotle

You don't have to do anything. People are constantly saying, "I have to do this or I have to that," but the reality is that nobody *has* to do anything. You choose to do everything that you do. Now you may be thinking, that is not true, I *have* to go to work or I *have* to pay my bills, but you really don't *have* to do either of these. The simple fact of the matter is that you don't have to do anything; you *choose* to do these things.

It's true; you don't have to go to work. Work is something that you choose to do either because you like having money or because you find it rewarding, but either way you make the choice to get up and go to your job each day. Nobody is forcing you to go to work. No one is forcing you to pay your bills. You choose to pay them in order to keep living the lifestyle that you have decided to live.

Likewise, nobody forces you to get angry or to lose your temper. Again, you choose to get angry or to lose your temper, and just as you choose to allow these things, you can also choose not to allow them. What lies in our power to do, it lies in our power not to do. You choose each and every one of your actions – all of them. There are no exceptions. The choice is 100% yours. You don't *have* to do anything. This is precisely why we are each responsible for all of our actions; we choose them therefore we are responsible for them. Think about this.

122

If you calm your own mind and discern the inner minds of others, that may be called the foremost art of war.
Shiba Yoshimasa

I have talked a lot about how the warrior should keep a calm and tranquil mind no matter what situation he may find himself in, but I haven't elaborated much on discerning the minds of others. This is another important skill for the warrior to learn. Shiba Yoshimasa calls the combination of these two skills the foremost art of war. They are both necessary for success. You have to develop, not only the ability to remain calm in adverse conditions, but the ability to sense when others mean you harm.

One of the advanced black belt tests in ninjutsu is called the sword test. The master stands behind a student, who is kneeling in meditation, with a bokken, ready to attack with a downward cut to the top of the head. The student is required to "sense" the attack and move to the side, avoiding the blow, at the exact moment of attack. If he moves too soon, he fails the test; if he moves too late, well he will have a tremendous headache.

Students who have successfully passed this test have a hard time putting into words how they avoided the blow of the sword. They simply say that they just moved. The purpose of this test is for the student to learn to sense the energy of someone who wants to do them harm. In order for this to work, the master has to truly be willing to hurt the student and he gives off this violent energy. Being able to sense danger before it comes is a great advantage to the warrior.

123

Patience is also a form of action.
Auguste Rodin

Being patient and waiting for the correct time to act can be confused with doing nothing, but there is a big difference in doing nothing and in patiently waiting for the right moment. In the movie *Rising Sun*, Sean Connery's character is being chased by some gangsters and his partner asks him, "Why are we running? We are the police!" Connery answered, "We aren't running, we're eluding." Subtle differences can make things totally different than they first appear.

Just as there is a difference between running away and eluding your enemy, there is also a difference in doing nothing and in patiently waiting for the right moment. As Rodin says, "Patience is also a form of action." Being patient is an action in itself and is different from doing nothing. Many times being patient is one of the hardest actions that the warrior can take. It takes a lot of discipline to be patient when you want to take care of things immediately.

Warriors had much rather take immediate physical action to set things straight, than to patiently wait for a more opportune time to act, but the warrior has to act from a place of inner wisdom, not from raw emotion. The warrior has to think rationally, not emotionally. When he knows inside that it is not time to act, he controls his urge to engage and instead elects to patiently wait. Patience is indeed a form of action, and one which requires great discipline to perfect. Practice patience and don't allow impatience to defeat you.

124

The wise man adapts himself to the circumstances.
Confucius

The warrior has a set of standards which he lives by and his code of honor has tenets that he is not willing to part with or break. His code of honor is an absolute in his life. Knowing this, you may think that the warrior's code of honor doesn't allow him to adapt to the circumstances, as Confucius teaches, but in reality it does allow the warrior to adapt himself to the circumstances as needed. Warrior honor is not black and white. It is much more complicated than that.

Adapting to the circumstances doesn't mean that the warrior has situational ethics. It doesn't mean that he picks and chooses when to live by his code of honor and when not to live by his code of honor. By adapting to the circumstances, Confucius is telling us to adapt our modes of action, not to compromise our standards or honor. For example, there is a time to take action and there is a time to wait. There is a time to speak up and a time to stay silent.

The warrior must be wise enough to adapt himself to the circumstance of the moment, not live by absolutes such as never allowing someone to shove him without severe consequences. Certain situations may call for the warrior to swallow his pride and walk away from an insult, instead of responding to it in a more direct manner, in order to accomplish his objective. Know your objective in each situation and adapt yourself as needed to accomplish your objective without compromising your honor or code of ethics. This is what Confucius was trying to teach us.

125

More satisfying by far, that many depend upon you, than that you depend upon anybody.
Baltasar Gracian

Don't be dependent on others. You shouldn't be dependent on anyone else for your protection or any other thing in your life. Have an independent spirit. Be self-reliant and responsible. Don't leave things to chance or depend on the honor or goodwill of others. Take control for yourself. Take the time to fix things in such a way that you know that you are safe because you have made yourself unassailable and self-reliant.

Spend the time and attention that it takes to guarantee your security and the safety of your family. You must make yourself un-attackable, as much as possible. Make sure that you and your family are safe from your enemies. Keep your reputation intact by being so honorable that no one would believe an attack on your character. Be in control. Don't leave things to chance. Build a defense that your enemy is unable to penetrate.

In today's world, even the weakest enemy can find ways to attack you. There are innumerable ways that your enemies can find to damage you, your family or your reputation. You can't depend on your enemy's good nature, character or ineptness to keep you safe. You have to make sure that your enemy has no choice in the matter, not because he is *unwilling*, but because he is *unable* to hurt you. Allow others to depend on you, and you depend on yourself. The warrior should work to become as self-sufficient as possible, in every area of his life.

126

Truth is not a matter of personal viewpoint.
Vernon Howard

The truth is the truth no matter what anyone thinks about it. Truth doesn't change because the majority doesn't agree with it or doesn't want it to be so. It is independent of all outside influences. Personal viewpoints play no part whatsoever in determining truth. People will debate the truth and then say things like, "It depends on how you look at it," but in reality, it doesn't matter how you "look at it." The truth doesn't change because you look at it one way or another.

The truth may seem elusive in many cases, but it is not. The truth simply is the truth, period. What is elusive, is people's ability to discern the truth, whether it is because of their prejudices, preconceived notions, or their simple refusal to accept the truth as the way things truly are. People tend to see what they want to see, whether it is the truth or not. Many people live in their own pre-constructed fantasy world where the truth holds little value.

This should not be the case for the warrior. The warrior can't afford to live in a fantasy world. He has to be rational and see things as they truly are in order to make rational decisions concerning his life. Refusing to see the truth for what it is, is just a form of escapism for those who do not want to deal with the realities of life. These are the people who will tell you violence never solved anything, while at the same time depending on the warrior to be prepared to defend their rights by violent means if necessary. Don't hide from the truth; embrace it and meet it head on with the determination of a warrior.

127

Many can speak words of wisdom; few can practice it themselves.
The Hitodadesa

Emerson said that a man's action is only a picture book of his creed. Do your actions match the lifestyle that you profess to live? Do you only speak like a man of wisdom, but live like a fool? Many people say one thing, but don't have the discipline to live the life that they endorse. Saying one thing and doing something else is the trademark of the hypocrite. If you are going to speak words of wisdom, you should practice them yourself. The warrior should not be hypocritical. If you are going to "talk the talk," you should be able to "walk the walk."

Don't talk about how noble the warrior lifestyle is and as soon as no one is looking, live in a manner that is totally contrary to it. If you believe that the warrior lifestyle is the way that you should live, and then live it. Don't say I'll try; just do it. It doesn't matter how many books you read on honor or how many lectures you listen to on character; if you don't utilize them in your life, they are worthless.

Don't be one of those people who dole out advice to everyone around them, but never put any of that wisdom to work in your own life. It is easy to tell other people how they should live. The true test is whether or not you can live the warrior lifestyle yourself. Few people can. That is why the true warrior is so rare, especially today. Dare to take your character seriously and put real wisdom to work in your life. Be one of the few, the honorable, and the noble – be a true warrior.

128

Put your heart, mind, intellect, and soul even to your smallest acts.
Swami Sivananda

If something is worth doing, it is worth doing well. It doesn't matter how small or insignificant the act is, concentrate on it and do it to the best of your ability. If you are working on your kata, focus entirely on your kata. Don't let your mind wander to other subjects. Don't think about what you are going to do later in the day or your "to-do" list. Focus on the task at hand. Put your entire self into whatever you happen to be doing at the time. This is what is meant by being in the present moment.

You have to concentrate on what you are doing right now, this very instant. If you are reading this and you are thinking about the movie on the television or you are thinking about your upcoming tournament, you are not putting your heart, mind, intellect, and soul into your reading. Consequently, you will not get as much out of your reading time as you should because you aren't 100% in the present moment. Take care of what you are doing at this moment in time, then move on to the next thing.

Marcus Aurelius stated the same thing when he said that you should do every act of your life as if it were your last. Slow down and take the time to make quality the cornerstone of everything that you do. If there is something more important on your mind than what you are doing, then stop what you are doing and go take care of the other thing first. To do two things at once is to do neither, or at least to do neither well.

129

A journey of a thousand miles begins with one step.
Lao Tzu

Some journeys are harder than others. Putting off the inevitable only extends the amount of time that it will take in order for you to get where you need to be. It doesn't matter how hard nor how long the journey is that you have to make; it starts with the first step. Don't delay your journey because of fear or dread. If it is a journey that you have to make, just get started and take it one step at a time.

Your decisions always bring with them consequences of one kind or another. This is just the way it is. Sometimes unwise, thoughtless decisions can have far-reaching consequences which we wish we didn't have to deal with, but deal with them we must. The consequences of our actions don't just disappear because we long for them to go away. You must take responsibility for your actions and deal with those consequences. The warrior has to take responsibility for all of his actions and the consequences which accompany those actions.

Sometimes the journey that our actions have set in motion can be a long, hard journey, but it still has to be traveled. Have the courage to face up to the road that you choose and walk it with honor. It doesn't matter if the road is long and hard, or if the road is short and easy, your journey still begins with one step. And, no matter how many bad, ill-thought out decisions you have made, you can still change your life. All it takes is making a firm decision to live life as it should be lived and it begins by taking that first step.

130

Convince the world by your character.
Chief John Ross

If someone attacks your character or your reputation, it really does very little good to enter into an argument over their accusations. Many times you only make things worse by addressing their attacks. In fact, this is a common ploy used by people of low character to bring attention to themselves when they are not deserving of attention. They will attack someone who is well known or someone of reputation just to get some attention. It is an example of the old adage, "No publicity is bad publicity."

The best way to handle such an attack is to ignore it. Don't add more fuel to the fire. Live your life in such a way that your reputation precedes you and that those who know you will defend your reputation without you having to get involved. This is what Chief John Ross means by convincing the world by your character. You let your own character defend you. By making the ideals of the warrior lifestyle a reality in your life, you are allowing your character to speak for you.

Of course this takes time. This is why you should strive to build and maintain the reputation of a man of honor and integrity. Once you have achieved a reputation as a man of character, and that reputation is built on a solid foundation, not on lies, then it will be hard for someone to successfully attack your character. The key here is that your character is true. You must live the warrior lifestyle, not pretend to live it. There is a big difference here. Build character, not the illusion of character. Be a true warrior.

131

What is of supreme importance in war is to attack the enemy's strategy.
Sun Tzu

Whether you are referring to war or business, if you want to win, you need to be able to counter your enemy's strategy. You first need to know exactly what your enemy's strategy is, in order to attack his strategy. Don't just shoot in the dark. You need factual knowledge concerning what he plans to do. Take the time to do a little research and find out who your enemy is and what makes him tick. You must know your enemy. Know his weaknesses and his strengths. Know what his goals are and what he wants to achieve and why. Gather as much information on him as possible.

Once you know your enemy well, you are ready to start thinking of ways to disrupt his strategy. Only after you understand your enemy, can you begin to devise a plan to attack his strategy. Attacking your enemy's strategy without doing your homework can backfire on you. You must be able to understand what is going on in your enemy's mind in order to plan your own strategy. You must know who he is and how he thinks in order to predict how he will react and what his next move will be.

Things are not always as they appear to be on the surface. In fact, they are seldom what they appear to be. You must work hard to get through all the layers and find out what your enemy's true purpose is. Don't just discover his strategy, but look deeper and find out why he has developed this strategy. What is his ultimate motivation? What is his ultimate objective? Once you know what his motivation is and what his objectives are, you are ready to develop a plan.

132

The secret of success is before attempting anything, be very clear about why you are doing it.
Guan Yin Tzu

You have to know your objective whenever you undertake anything. If you don't know why you are doing something, then it will not be long until you start to wonder why you are spending time in this endeavor. Be clear about what you want and why you are spending your time as you are. Takuan Soho wrote that, "You must carefully consider the merits of any action." Is this specific action worth your time?

If you are putting in hours each day training with weights and in martial arts, you had better know why you are putting in this sweat equity. Being unsure about why you are working so hard will only lead to a lack of motivation, and eventually discontinuing your training. There has to be a good reason behind your actions in order to stay motivated. This is one reason that you need specific goals. Goals give you a clear picture about your objectives and keep you motivated to achieve them.

Once you know your objectives, stay focused on them. Focused energy is much more powerful than dispersed energy. Concentrate on achieving your goals. Think about them. Visualize yourself completing the task at hand. Read things which help keep you motivated. Knowing that you are training for that life-and-death encounter will help keep you going when you don't really feel motivated to train. Always keep the "why" fresh in your mind and your motivation will remain high.

133

Chance is a word void of sense; nothing can exist without a cause.
Voltaire

I have talked a little about not leaving your life to chance. The warrior should try as much as it is within his power, to be prepared for whatever may come into his life. Being unprepared is tantamount to leaving your life up to the winds of fate. Sun Tzu stated in his classic book, *The Art of War*, that you should not rely on the likelihood of your enemy not coming, but on your own readiness to receive him.

If you are not prepared to make yourself unassailable to a possible enemy, it is not chance or bad luck that causes your misfortune when you are attacked. It is the fact that you caused your own injury by your lack of preparation and awareness. You did not make yourself unassailable and therefore when some thug attacked you, you were injured. Nothing happens by chance. Everything has its cause and effect.

Both your invincibility and your vulnerability depend on you. You make the decision. There is no such thing as luck. You may disagree and think that it was just pure bad luck that some thug picked you as a target, but you were the one who put yourself in a certain location, at a specific time, and on top of that, unprepared to deal with the threat. No matter what the end product may turn out to be, you can be sure that there was some cause that preceded it. Nothing can exist without a cause; everything happens for a reason.

134

Able to be calm, then able to respond.
Xunzi

It is vital for the warrior to keep his mind calm. Nothing good ever comes from panicking. Panicking, whether in a physical encounter or in a medical emergency, only leads to mistakes and irrational thought processes. In critical situations, you must keep your wits about you. These are times when you have to be able to think rationally and clearly in order to respond in an efficient manner.

Although it is essential to stay calm and focused in high stress situations, this is only half of the equation. You must also be able and willing to respond to the circumstances which you find yourself in at the present moment. It doesn't do much good to stay calm and at the same time, just sit and do nothing to alleviate the problem. Critical situations require action, not just tranquil composure.

You must be able to balance these two in order to correctly handle any state of affairs, whether it is disciplining your children or defending your life in a violent street encounter. The warrior can't afford to lose his temper when confronted by a violent thug, and he can't afford to panic when his son has cut himself with a sharp knife. No matter what position he finds himself in, the warrior has to respond with calm self-assurance and take control of the situation.

135

Listening to only one side creates prejudice.
Japanese Maxim

The warrior has to base his judgments and his decisions on the truth. There is no merit in self-deceit or in coming to a conclusion without having all the necessary information. This is exactly what you are doing if you make decisions after hearing only one side of the story. Listening to one side of an argument leads to making a decision based on prejudicial information. This is why the judge in a courtroom listens to both the prosecution and the defense. Every coin has two sides.

If someone asked you to describe a silver dollar and you only described the front side, you have only given one viewpoint. When that person looks at the flip side, he will see a totally different design than the one you described to him. Armed with the information that you gave him, he may argue that this coin is not a silver dollar because it doesn't look like the coin that you described to him. His argument would be wrong because it was based on incomplete information.

You only gave him half of the information which he needed to come to an intelligent conclusion. The same principle goes for discerning the facts when other people are giving you details as they see them. If you listen to only one side of the story, you are only getting information from one person's point of view. You need to listen to both sides, examine all the information and then make decisions based on facts and truth, not prejudice and ignorance. Take the time to get to the truth before you put your honor on the line.

136

Regardless of social class,
there should be no discourteous behavior.
Tomida Dairai

Everyone should be treated with respect and in a courteous manner. It doesn't matter who they are or what their social class may be. Being courteous says more about you than the person you are interacting with at the time. It shows that you have standards that you adhere to, and that you live by those standards at all times, not just when you are trying to impress someone or speaking to someone "important."

Does this mean that everyone deserves your respect? Absolutely not! To quote Clint Eastwood, "Deserve has nothing to do with it." It doesn't matter whether or not the person you are talking to deserves to be respected or not. Deserve has nothing to do with it; you treat others with respect because that is who you are. The warrior lives by his own standards, independent of what other people do or don't do. Their actions don't determine his manners.

Too many people treat people, who they see as "below" them, in a different manner than they do people who they consider important. This type of situational etiquette is insincere. In actuality, they have no more respect for the "important" people than they do for the "lower class" people. They are only putting on a show for the people who they consider important enough to see the act. Insincerity is not a trait that the warrior should foster. Be courteous to everyone who crosses your path. Be of noble mind.

137

In strategy, secrecy is esteemed.
Japanese Proverb

There is a big difference between keeping things private and being insincere or misleading. Many people believe that they have to tell everyone their every thought. This is not a wise philosophy to live by, whether you are just casually chatting or in the middle of a business negotiation. There are many things which should be kept secret. This doesn't mean that you aren't being sincere. It simply means that you are being wise.

Not everything is everyone else's business. It is good strategy to keep private things secret. Don't share all of your thoughts or be too open with all of your plans. You should be careful what you share and keep most things to yourself. Many plans have been ruined because someone disclosed too much information. People talk and they will repeat what you say.

If you disclose your line of attack, you can be sure that you are giving others the opportunity to prepare to defeat your strategy. By not keeping your strategy secret, you are actually weakening your line of attack, or in the case of the warrior, your defense. The masters of old were extremely careful not to disclose too much information concerning their favorite techniques, even to their senior students. By divulging too much information, you are actually putting yourself in danger. Think about this.

138

Always think in terms of what the other person wants.
James Van Fleet

I have already stated several times that the warrior should always try to resolve potential conflicts without letting things deteriorate into a physical encounter. He should use his mind and his verbal skills to stop disagreements from getting out of hand. What matters in these circumstances is that the warrior achieves his objectives, not that he looks tough or that he looks like a big shot.

The way to accomplish this is to think in terms of what the other person wants. Why is this person upset or angry? What is it that he wants to have happen in this situation? What would it take to smooth things over with him? These are all questions that the warrior has to be able to answer on the spot in order to successfully take control before things get physical. Your objective is for you and those around you to walk away unharmed and safe, not to put this guy in his place.

The answers to the questions above give you the information that you need to accomplish your objective. It may take little more than an apology to settle the whole issue. It doesn't matter if there is nothing that you should apologize for or not, your objective is to walk away from this incident having defeated your opponent, not to prove that you are in the right. After all, you already know that you are in the right; it doesn't matter whether or not this guy agrees with you. Find out what the other guy wants and give it to him if it can be done without compromising your honor. A victory in disguise is still a victory.

139

No battle's won in bed.
The Havamal

It is easy to start to think that you have reached the peak of your training and to think that you have all the skills that you need to handle whatever street punk you may meet. It is very tempting to skip your training when you allow these kinds of thoughts to enter your mind, but remember, victory is not gained through idleness. Every day you skip your training, there is some thug out there training hard, just waiting for the chance to use his skills against you or some other unsuspecting soul.

You never reach the point where you no longer need to train to keep yourself in shape and to keep your skills sharp. Realize that the punks in the street will have little mercy for you when and if you have to confront them. You have to be ready. You have to keep your skills sharp and ready even if you feel that you will not need them. Once you decide that you no longer need to train, your skills will start to regress; you will be less prepared to meet trouble.

You never know when you will be called on to use your training in a life-or-death situation. If you aren't ready, it could cost you your life or the life of someone you love. Be prepared. Don't become complacent in your training. No battle is won is bed, but many battles can be lost in bed. Laziness and complacency have no place in the warrior lifestyle. Replace the urge towards lethargy with the discipline of a warrior. Always remember that somewhere out there, there is some thug who is honing his skills for the day when your paths cross.

140

Be slow of tongue and quick of eye.
Cervantes

In simple terms, this quote from Cervantes boils down to keep your mouth shut and pay attention, although Cervantes put it a little more elegantly than that. The majority of people that I observe today, love to hear themselves talk. They never really listen to the people around them or pay any attention to what they are saying. Their mind is always focused on the next witty thing that they can say to make themselves sound intelligent or humorous.

Rarely do these types of people learn anything from the people around them because they simply do not pay attention to the conversation. They don't engage their mind or put any thought into what is being said. As a consequence, they also tend to put their foot in their mouth on a frequent basis, saying things which either do not make sense or which are inappropriate, just to have something to say.

This should not describe the warrior. The warrior should use his words sparingly. He should spend more time listening and observing, than babbling away. Using your words cautiously and thinking about what you are saying before you actually say it, are two traits which the warrior needs to develop. These are traits of the wise man and the man of substance, and should be traits of the true warrior. Always be wary about what you say and how you say it. Being careless with your speech can cause you many unnecessary problems. Be slow of tongue, quick of eye, and quick of mind.

141

Lower your voice and strengthen your argument.
Lebanon Proverb

As I walk down the hallways of the school, it is not unusual at all to hear teachers yelling at the top of their lungs in a feeble attempt to gain control of an unruly class. When I peek into these loud rooms, I almost always find that the students view the teacher's outburst as humorous. They have caused that teacher to lose control of his or her emotions, and in a sense, they have won the battle.

In contrast, when I am in the classroom, I hardly ever have the need to raise my voice, yet my classes are always in control and usually on task. These are the same students, in the same school, in the same hallway, and adhering to the same discipline policy. So why do these students act one way in one class and another way in a classroom right next door? I wondered this myself and I asked one of the rougher students about this one day. His answer was very interesting.

He informed me that he knew that Mr. X would not follow through on what he said whether he was yelling or speaking in a normal tone. He went on to say that he knew that I meant exactly what I said and it didn't matter if I whispered it or announced it to the entire class. This student went on to summarize the situation in the following way, "We have respect for you and we don't respect Mr. X. You don't pull your punches and everyone knows it." When you speak with authority, you don't have to yell and get all worked up to get your point across. People can sense whether or not you mean what you say. Just say what you mean, and mean what you say.

142

You always win by not saying the things you don't need to say.
Chinese Proverb

There is a difference in not revealing everything that you know, and in being deceitful. Shakespeare wrote that men of few words are the best men, and this is something that the warrior should consider. Not only are men of few words the best men, but they are also in a more secure position as far as their life goes. Many, many people get themselves in trouble by talking too much and saying things which, not only don't need to be said, but which could actually cause their downfall.

Keep the majority of your thoughts to yourself. Just because you think something or you believe something, doesn't mean that you have to share it with someone else. Be selective about, not only who you talk to, but also what you say. Most people love to talk and do so without giving much thought to what they say. Even if they have the best intentions about not repeating something that you have told them, many times they will do so anyway without thinking.

You always win by not saying the things that you shouldn't say. It is much easier to restrain your urge to talk than it is to clean up a mess that you have made by saying too much. Keep private things private. Don't talk without first giving some thought to what you want to communicate and the consequences of what you are about to say. Think before you speak and have a purpose behind your words.

143

Seek the counsel of the aged, for their eyes have looked on the faces of the years and their ears have hearkened to the voices of Life.
Kahlil Gibran

People used to honor the elders for their wisdom and knowledge, but today many people simply try to send them away so they aren't bothered by their needs. Many people today seem to forget that older people have been through many of the same things that we go through, and they have wisdom concerning how to deal with the problems that we are currently dealing with today. It is silly to have a resource available to help you and refuse to use that resource.

If you are lucky enough to know an older person who can give you advice and guidance, be smart enough to listen to their counsel. Many times they know what they are talking about, and if they are your family members, you have a filial duty to spend time with them and talk to them. You should never act on someone's advice until you feel that it is right, but as Gibran went on to say, "Even if their counsel is displeasing to you, pay heed to them."

It never hurts to listen to the opinions of others. Someone else may think of something that has eluded you, especially if that person has many more years of experience. Of course, not all elderly people are wise. Fools grow old too. Wise men are rare regardless of their age, but when you find a wise man, listen to what he has to say, whether he is five years old or 105 years old. Seek the wisdom of the elders and put it to use in your life. The wise man will learn from the mistakes and experiences of others.

144

Don't follow any advice, no matter how good, until you feel as deeply in your spirit as you think in your mind that the counsel is wise.
David Seabury

The wise man listens to the thoughts of others, but always makes his own decisions. Ultimately, you are the only person responsible for your actions. Nobody else will be held accountable for the choices which you make. Since you, and you alone are responsible for the choices that you make, shouldn't you actually be the one who decides what those choices are. Make sure that your actions are based on your choices, not the choices of other people.

It is good to listen to the advice and admonitions of others at times, but don't automatically take the advice of others to be the gospel or to be more enlightened than your own thoughts. Meditate on the right choice until you feel deep in your spirit that you know which road to take. Don't simply rely on your mind to figure things out. Spend time in quiet meditation. Clear your mind and listen to your intuition or your spirit.

Buddha taught the same principle to his followers. He said that you shouldn't believe anything merely because someone tells you this or that. You should examine things for yourself, think about them, and not act on them until you know inside that they are right; then act on what you know is right. The warrior knows that he is solely responsible for his decisions in life, and therefore he is not content to act without giving thought to his actions beforehand. Listen to the counsel of the wise, but make your own decisions.

145

Do not let trifles disturb your tranquility of mind. Ignore the inconsequential.
Grenville Kleiser

The warrior should strive to do the best that he can do in every area of his life. It is a part of his nature to try to make every part of his life as perfect as possible. He strives for excellence in every area of his life, but no matter how hard he tries, there will always be times when things will not go as planned. Everyone has stumbling blocks that they have to maneuver around on their journey. Don't focus on the stumbling blocks; focus on your actions and your response to these challenges.

Everything matters, but not everything is important enough to get upset over. Don't let these small glitches disturb your mind. If something is inconsequential, don't spend time thinking about it, and even if something is momentous, don't let it rob you of your peace of mind. Whether the challenge that you have to face is small or monumental, maintain your composure and strive to keep a tranquil mind. Worry and stress are worthless in your quest to overcome your problems.

I'm not suggesting that you just ignore your problems and hope that they somehow mysteriously disappear. Things don't change simply because you don't want to deal with them. What I am saying is don't sweat the small stuff. Not only should you not sweat the small stuff, but don't let the larger things bother you either. Simply do the best that you can do in each moment to deal with the issue at hand and move on to the next moment. The way of the warrior is in rational action, not immobilized worry.

146

Deliberate often – Decide once.
Latin Proverb

The warrior has to be decisive. He has to spend time meditating on his values and his standards, and he has to know who he is deep down inside. This information gives him a moral compass as to how to live his life and how to make the important decisions that have to be made throughout his journey. Everyone has important decisions which have to be made in their life. Your choices determine your destiny.

It is vital that you make the correct choices because every choice carries with it a set of consequences. For this reason you have to look at all the possibilities when you are deliberating what you should and should not do. Examine the pros and the cons. Look at the possible consequences for each choice. Don't rush your decisions. Take your time when possible, and don't make a decision until you feel confident on the inside that your decision is correct.

Once you feel that you have made the best decision that you possibly can make, stick with it. The time for debating the issue has passed. You have spent time meditating on your options, you have thought about the different outcomes, and you have made the best decision that you could make. Have confidence that you have done the best that you could do to make an intelligent decision. Don't second guess yourself over and over again. This only causes doubt and stress to cloud your mind. Deliberate often – decide once, and then stand firm on your decision.

147

Think like a man of action, act like a man of thought.
Thomas Mann

How does a man of action think? Well, to start with, he thinks about what can be done to solve the problem at hand or to make things better. The man of action is a go-getter. He doesn't wait to see what others think or depend on others to step up while he minds his own business. The man of action wants to get things done and make things right. His thoughts center on accomplishing his goals, and doing so in the most efficient manner possible. "Do it now" is his mantra.

The man of thought on the other hand, likes to think things through before he makes a move. He examines all the possible outcomes of his actions and tries to see the situation from all sides. Realizing that there is more to most things than meets the eye, he delves deeper into things in order to develop a true understanding of them. He searches for the truth so he can make decisions based on facts rather than emotions. Justice and honor are foremost on his mind.

The warrior should find balance between the traits of the two types of men. Think like a man of action, but act like a man of thought. Be ready for action and know what action is needed should things come to that, but at the same time, be calm, collected and rational like a man of thought. Think things through before you speak or act. Don't be rash. Integrate these traits into one and find a sense of balance between the two. A calm, rational mind which is always ready for action is a trait of the true warrior.

148

Justice is the virtue of warriorhood, the root of martial arts.
Nakae Toju

Justice is the root of martial arts, and it is also the root of warriorhood. Justice means fairness or reasonableness, especially in the way that you treat other people. Without justice, you are missing an essential part of the warrior lifestyle and an essential part of the character which is necessary to become a true warrior. If the root is bad, the branches and the leaves will also be bad. This is true for plants and trees, and it is also true for your martial arts and your life as a warrior.

The warrior is dedicated to justice. This is one of the main forces behind his willingness to serve and to protect others. He cannot be indifferent while others around him are forced to endure the injustice of those more powerful. It would be against his nature to take no action when justice is at stake. Duty requires that the warrior support justice in as much as it is in his power to make a difference. It takes courage to stand against injustice, but courage is a trademark of the warrior.

Martial arts must have at its root the seed of justice or they become self-serving. Once martial arts become self-serving, they become tools for lesser men, men with low character, men who can no longer call themselves warriors. It is not knowledge of the martial arts which makes a man a warrior, but knowledge of the martial arts which have grown from the roots of justice, honor and character, which lead to the warrior lifestyle. Strive to make sure that the roots of your martial arts and your character are strong.

149

Do not forget great kindness, even for a single meal.
Emperor Wen Di

People in today's world seem to feel that the world "owes" them something. They have the attitude that they are somehow special and deserving. Gratitude is something that many people pay lip service to, but never really understand what it actually means. Sure, it is common to hear someone say "Thank you," but are they actually grateful for the kindness that they have received?

You should remember that no one "owes" you anything in this world. They don't have to hold the door open for you. They don't have to return your lost dog. They don't have to do anything for you at all. It is only out of the kindness of their heart that people do nice things for other people, and you should be sincerely grateful when someone does do something nice or kind for you.

As a teacher, I see ungratefulness on a daily basis, especially in younger people. Someone will do them a favor or go out of their way to help them, and they couldn't care less. When I lecture them about how lucky they are that someone was willing to help them, I hear things such as "Well, it didn't cost them anything," or "It was no big deal." People have lost the attitude of gratefulness.

This should not be the case for the warrior. The true warrior knows that if someone does something for him, he is indebted to that person. At the very least, he should show sincere gratitude, but what's more, he owes that person for their kindness. Don't take small acts of kindness for granted; be grateful for what you have and for what others do for you.

150

If you are always getting angry, you will turn your nature against the Way.
Bodhidharma

Emotions have more of an effect on the body than most people realize. Your emotions affect your body chemistry, and your body chemistry can affect everything from the way that you feel to the way that you think. Science is just starting to scratch the surface of how your emotions affect your body, but what they do know is that negative emotions have a negative effect on your body.

Anger is one of the negative emotions which can have a negative effect on your body. Not only does uncontrollable anger affect your body chemistry, but it can also become addictive. That's right, anger can be addictive, or to be more exact, the different chemicals released by the body during anger can be addictive. Anger produces certain chemical effects in the body, which in turn produce a specific feeling.

If you continue to allow yourself to get angry over and over until it becomes a habit, it will hinder you in the goals that you have set for yourself as far as the warrior lifestyle goes. You have to takes steps to control your anger and break this pattern. The same goes for any negative emotion which you allow to become a habit. Negative emotions lead to negative energy, and adversely affect your body. Don't permit them to play a part in your life. Take control of your anger and other negative emotions today.

151

In the midst of men who hate us, let us live without hatred.
The Dhammapada

The old adage that you fight fire with fire is a good analogy for many things, but it is not for hatred. *The Dhammapada* states that hatred can only be combated with love, not more hate. When hatred is met with more hatred, it only fosters a continuing cycle of hatred among men. Fight hate with love, but take care that you realize what this means and that you think about this rationally.

You are responsible for your actions, not someone else's actions. If someone has a malicious hatred towards you, this doesn't give you a license to hate them back. You must still walk the path of warriorhood by the same standards of integrity and honor, no matter how someone else acts. Too many people live with the idea that if someone crosses them, the gloves are off and anything goes.

The warrior does not have the liberty to put his standards to the side just because someone wrongs him. He is required to live by his code of honor. Even if everyone around him hates him, he still must live without allowing hatred to be a part of his mindset. This doesn't mean that he doesn't fight back when action is required. Warriors can use their martial arts skills against an enemy without hating that enemy. The fact that the warrior tries all else before resorting to violence, attests to the reality that the warrior is not acting out of hatred, but out of necessity. Think about this.

152

Take a deep breath of life and consider how it should be lived.
Don Quixote's Creed

Don Quixote's creed contains a lot of wisdom that we can all benefit from if we will only slow down and listen to it. Slow down and take a look at your life and consider how it should be lived. It seems that the majority of people just go through life randomly reacting to whatever comes their way. They don't appear to have any set ideas about how they should live their life. They simply go through the motions day by day.

The warrior should take the time to retire to a quiet place and meditate on his life and how he should live his life. He shouldn't just go through the motions, but instead he should consider the value of life and how quickly it disappears. Life should be lived to the fullest each and every day, and not only lived, but lived with character and honor.

Take time to consider how your life should be lived. How should a true warrior spend his time? Are you truly living your life to the fullest or do you walk through your days on autopilot? If your self-examination reveals that you haven't been living life to the fullest, it is time to make a change. Don't wait another day; start living today.

Determine what it is that you want from life and what you need to do to manifest the kind of life that you want. Don't wander through life with no idea of what you want or who you want to be. Sit down and map out your life. Determine how your life will be lived, and then live it, every day.

153

A hero in old age never lets go of his principles.
Cao Cao

The warrior lifestyle is built on specific principles which the warrior makes his own. These principles actually become a part of who he is as a man. They are not something that he uses when he needs them and then puts them in a closet until the next time that he finds he needs to pull them out and apply them. The principles of warriorship become as much a part of the warrior as his arm or his leg. They become ingrained in his spirit.

Knowing this, the above quote by Cao Cao appears very obvious. The hero doesn't let go of his principles as he ages. His principles actually become more embedded in his spirit as he gets older. They are a part of who he has become over many years of training and learning from his mistakes and his triumphs. The aging warrior has learned the value of character, integrity and honor, and knows the importance of maintaining his standards.

He would consider it ridiculous to let go of his principles after many years spent honing them to perfection. Instead of letting go of his principles, the warrior in his old age elects to pass on his wisdom to those who will listen. He is able to see the mistakes which the younger people are making because he has seen the same mistakes before, and he knows what must be done to correct and deal with these mistakes.

The wise man will listen to the aging warrior's wisdom and learn. With age comes insight, especially in those who have been wise enough to develop the traits of the warrior. Listen to their wisdom and learn from their experience.

154

Faces we see, hearts we know not.
Spanish Proverb

Do you really know who someone else is or what someone else thinks? It's not likely. You only get to know and see what someone allows you to know and see, and this may not be reality, but rather a mere charade. Most people are very careful about the image that they portray to everyone else. Only a handful of people are allowed to know the real person, the person without the protective shield that is up when we are around others.

This is just a human characteristic that the majority of people come by naturally, and because of this trait, it is important that you learn to "read" people. You have to be able to discern what is really going on in their heart. This takes practice and skill, but it can be done. There are many books on the market which go into detail about how to read people's expressions, body language, and small tell signs.

Just as poker players learn to read their opponents, the warrior should make it part of his training to learn how to read the people around him. He should become an expert in the art of reading his fellow man. Learn how to tell if someone is bluffing, lying, being deceitful, or being completely honest. Learn the small eye movements and hand gestures that are unconscious and common among most humans. Develop that x-ray vision that allows you to see past the face and into the heart and mind of those that you meet.

155

It is essential to cultivate the warrior spirit.
Saito Totsudo

What is the warrior spirit? This 17th century Confucian scholar's teachings, as translated by Thomas Cleary in his book *Training the Samurai Mind*, states that cultivating the "warrior spirit" was an essential part of being a samurai. He taught that even if you have all the strength and training that is needed to be a warrior, they will be of no use if you lack the warrior spirit. According to Totsudo, it is not the external strength which truly matters, but the internal strength – the strength of the spirit.

The warrior spirit is based on courage. It is the courage to stand up for justice and for what is right, no matter what the odds. You can only develop this deep seated courage if you truly know that you are in the right. If you have doubts about whether or not you are right, then those doubts will affect you on the inside and you will have doubts concerning the legitimacy of your stand. After all, if you aren't completely convinced that you are right, how can you stand with conviction against someone who takes the other side of the issue?

Firmness and decisiveness are the legs which courage stands upon. Doubt is the stumbling block which causes courage to falter. Courage is the foundation of the warrior spirit. The traits of firmness, decisiveness, and courage can only be rightly obtained through meditating on what is right and your own personal code of honor. Once you have determined you will live by your own standards and you are clear about what those standards are, then all that is left is to have the courage to live by those standards.

156

My enemy is not the man who wrongs me, but the man who means to wrong me.
Democritus

Every enemy has the capability to disrupt your life, some in a small way and others to a much larger capacity, but not that many of them go to the effort to cause you harm. The fact that you don't openly see enemies attacking you physically, verbally or discreetly behind your back, doesn't mean that you do not have any enemies. It simply means that your enemies are not malevolent enough or energetic enough to make the effort to cause you harm, but their lack of effort should not be mistaken for a lack of malevolence toward you.

As Democritus taught, just because a man does you no harm, it doesn't mean he is not your enemy. You have to look deeper than that. You have to read between the lines. Your enemy is not only the man who wrongs you, but also the man who longs to see you wronged. He is the man who is happy when you are hit with misfortune, the man who celebrates your downfall. Your enemy is he who wishes you calamity, even if he doesn't have the courage to openly state the fact.

Be careful who you trust. You don't always know who your enemies are. They are not always those who openly oppose you. The enemies of a good man are usually not men of character and backbone. They are more likely to be men of low character who lack the courage to openly come against you. Instead, they find it easier to simply sit back and think malicious thoughts of your ruin. Be wise and learn to read people's spirits. Be careful who you trust.

157

The wise live among people, but are indifferent to their praise or blame.
Chuang Tzu

People are fickle. They will sing your praises one day, and they will turn on you like a pack of wolves the next day. Throughout history, people have shown this same erratic behavior, and sages have always taught us, just as Chuang Tzu taught, to be indifferent to the praise or blame of the masses. Let their praise and blame roll off of your back just as rain beads up and rolls off of a newly waxed car.

This advice sounds easy enough to do. After all, it doesn't take much effort to ignore what other people say, right? Well, this is another piece of wisdom that is easier said than done. It is very enjoyable and ego-boosting to have people praising your work and patting you on the back. It is a very pleasurable experience for people to tell you how great you are or how smart you are.

Likewise, it is a very uncomfortable feeling to have people attacking you and blaming you for this or that. It can be very stressful to have people harass you verbally. Being indifferent to the public's opinions, either positive or negative, is something which has to be learned and perfected. It doesn't come naturally.

Just remember that the same people who cheer for you today, would cheer just as loudly if you were about to be hanged. Don't seek the approval of the public. Seek the approval of men of wisdom and honor. These are men whose opinions actually have substance. Above all, seek to live according to your own principles. Only you truly know if you are worthy of praise or blame.

158

Cultivate the root.
Confucius

No matter what the warrior is studying or trying to understand, he should always strive to cultivate the root. Confucius taught that if you cultivate the root, the leaves and the branches will take care of themselves. This means that if you want to truly become proficient in any art or any profession, you first have to learn the basics of that art or that profession. You can't have a strong tree without first having strong roots.

Too many people today want to skip this vital step in the process of the martial arts. They want to learn the flashy kicks or the "secret" moves, but they are not very interested in learning the basics. They find the basics kind of boring and tedious. The novice martial artist wants to learn to do what they see in the movies and on television, not practice stances or basic kicking and punching techniques. It seems that they want to grow branches and leaves with no roots.

This is not the way of nature and it is not the way of the warrior. You have to learn to stand before you learn to walk, and you have to learn to walk before you learn to run. This is just the natural progression of things. Learning a martial art should follow the same natural progression as everything else in nature. You must cultivate the root first; don't skip this essential part of your training. Without strong, deep roots, it takes very little adversity to kill a plant or to expose a martial artist's weaknesses.

159

Muddy water, let stand, becomes clear.
Lao Tzu

As I have said before, stress, worry, anxiety, and fear can cloud your mind. When these emotions are allowed to take control of your mind, it is hard to see things clearly or make good decisions. Your mind can't focus and will begin to become "muddy" if you will. It is hard to think rationally when your mind is bombarded with these emotions. Just as a crystal clear lake can become muddy when the sediment at the bottom is disturbed, your mind will become "muddy" when it is disturbed.

So what do you do to clear your mind when it has become cloudy from these emotions? Do the same thing as the lake does to become clear again – nothing. The lake simply waits for the muddy particles to settle back where they belong, and once again the lake becomes crystal clear. You should do the same thing. Quit thinking about the issue at hand. Just put that subject on the shelf for a while. Do something else like meditate, work in the garden, or work out.

It really doesn't matter what you do, as long as you get your mind off of the problem that is causing these emotions to cloud your thinking. Just get away from it and allow the "mud" to settle. When you come back, your mind, like the lake, will have cleared up and you will be able to see things differently. Once again, you will be able to think rationally and intelligently, the way the warrior should think. The key here is to be patient. You can't make the mud settle back to the bottom of the lake by pushing it back down; it has to settle on its own, at its own pace.

160

Those who do good because they want to be seen to be good are not good.
Lieh Tzu

Why does the warrior seek to do what he considers right according to his code of ethics? Is it because he knows that others expect him to be upstanding and live with honor? Does he only do the right thing to impress others or when others are observing his actions? No, the warrior seeks to live by his code of ethics because deep down inside he is committed to living up to the strict standards which he has set for himself.

He is not concerned with whether or not others approve or disapprove of his actions, as long as he knows inside his spirit that he is living according to the code which he has decided to make his own. The warrior lives the lifestyle of the warrior because that is who he is, not because he wants to impress someone or he wants to brag about his ethics. He walks the path of justice because he has made a firm decision to do so.

Not everyone shares this dedication to doing what is right. Many people only do good because they want to impress others; they want to make a reputation for themselves that will help them climb the social ladder of success. They want to be seen as good, but they really have no burning desire to be good. In fact, when it comes down to it, they really don't care about justice. They care about what is best for their own goals and status. They aren't truly good, upstanding people, but only appear good. Don't be a hypocrite. Live the ideals that you subscribe to, whether in public or private.

161

Honor is central to warriorship.
Forrest E. Morgan

Several people have disagreed with my assessment that the warrior is more than someone who is trained and experienced in the art of warfare. I maintain that to be a true warrior you have to have more than martial arts training or military training; you also have to have character, integrity and honor. In fact, according to Forrest E. Morgan in his book *Living the Martial Way*, honor is one of the key traits of warriorship.

Honor is basically your personal integrity. It is having strong moral character and strength, and adherence to ethical principles. If someone is lacking these character traits, can we truly say that he is a warrior, or is he just someone who has been trained to fight and kill? There are many members of street gangs who know how to fight and are efficient killers, but are they truly warriors?

Well, by now you know that my answer to that is a resounding no! It takes much more to be a warrior than the willingness to fight. True warriorship involves a lifestyle which is much more complicated than that. It involves honor and living a life of service to others. It involves character and integrity, and a dedication to justice. And yes, at times it does involve being willing and able to fight, but fighting is only a small piece of the warrior lifestyle. You can be a fighter without being a warrior, but you can't be a warrior without honor.

162

Rediscover natural compassion.
Lao Tzu

I recently wrote in my blog that the warrior is naturally a compassionate human being and received several critical comments questioning this statement. Many of my readers asked how I could possibly say that warriors are compassionate when they train to fight and are willing to hand out some severe damage to other people. The answer is that the warrior has a heart for justice and service. Only someone with compassion is willing to put their life on the line to protect others or to fight for justice.

If you do not have compassion for other people, you don't care if they are being abused, mugged, or beaten. Without compassion, you are not willing to stand up for those who can't stand up for themselves. Why would anyone in their right mind consider serving others without any compensation or many times without even a thank you? They wouldn't unless they had some deep seated compassion and true concern for the welfare of others.

Some of my readers have stated that compassion will get the warrior killed, but this is not true. Lack of judgment about the right time and right place to act on your compassion will get you killed, but compassion is a must for the true warrior. When a terrorist is driving a car bomb towards you, it is not the time to be compassionate to this human being. This doesn't mean that you aren't compassionate, but that you have good judgment. A kill-or-be-killed situation is not the time to be compassionate to your enemy, but it doesn't mean that the warrior lacks compassion. Rediscover natural compassion and develop the wisdom to know when and how to express that compassion.

163

Never be easily drawn into a fight.
Gichin Funakoshi

The warrior should only fight when all other options have been exhausted. By "fight" I mean an all out, no holds barred encounter. There may be times when you find that you have to restrain someone or prevent someone from continuing on a belligerent path, but this can be done without the warrior using the full extent of his power. This is different than actually fighting, and calls for wisdom and discretion.

If you encounter some drunk who is a bit out of control, pushing and shoving someone, some simple restraint may be all that is called for, not the total obliteration of this guy. Another example would be if your son is high on drugs and out of control, you certainly wouldn't want to hurt him, but it may take some restraint or a nice stern punch to snap him back into reality. These are just two examples of where you may have to restrain someone or pull your punches because the situation calls for a moderate response.

This is not the same as a true fight. A fight is a serious situation where you have no choices left, and where someone is going to get hurt. This kind of encounter is a grave situation and should be taken seriously. Never allow yourself to be easily drawn into this kind of situation. Always try your best to avoid fighting and to resolve things peacefully if at all possible. You should stay in control of the situation; don't be manipulated into a fight. Be smart enough to maintain your focus on your objective and don't let your emotions get involved.

164

Discipline, not desire,
determines your destiny.
Bud Malmstrom

You can want something very badly, but that doesn't mean that you will achieve it. It takes more than desire to achieve your goals; it takes desire and discipline. Desire by itself is little more than wishing, and wishing for something will get you nowhere. Sitting around and daydreaming about becoming a black belt will not earn you either the skills of a practicing black belt or the rank of black belt. You have to take action to get what you want.

This is where discipline comes into play. You have to have discipline to achieve your goals. Without discipline, your actions will be sporadic and inconsistent. It takes discipline to live the lifestyle of the warrior. It takes discipline to achieve any goal that is worth achieving, and the goals that you achieve or fail to achieve, determine your destiny. Desiring something without disciplining yourself to attain it is like wanting money but refusing to go to work.

You have to work for what you want in this life. If you want a black belt, you have to have the discipline to work for that black belt several days a week, almost every week for several years. This takes discipline. If you want to walk the path of the warrior, you have to discipline yourself to develop the character traits of the warrior. You have to discipline yourself to live by a stricter code of honor than the average man on the street. It takes discipline, not simply the desire.

165

Remember how lucky you are to live in a time of peace and plenty, but prepare for worse times.
Code of the Samurai

Most of us live a peaceful life. In our society today, unless you are in the military or work in law enforcement, you most likely live in peace and plenty. Even those in our country who are on the bottom of the economic pecking order live a life of plenty when compared to people in many third world countries. We live in a time of peace and abundance in the United States today, but there is no guarantee that things will always remain as they are today.

The *Code of the Samurai* points this out to us. The samurai saw both times of peace and prosperity and times of war which ravished their country. They knew from experience that things can change, and change quickly. Times of peace and plenty can turn into times of chaos and anarchy in the blink of an eye. It is wise to be prepared for the possibility of a time when things will not be so peaceful and when prosperity turns to scarcity.

You lose nothing by preparing for bad times during the good times. When things are good and you are surrounded by blessings, it is time to think of defending yourself against the change of tide. Be disciplined enough to save some of your wealth for a rainy day. Keep yourself physically fit and your martial arts skills sharp. Be wise enough to realize that nothing lasts forever, good or bad. Enjoy the good times while they last, but at the same time prepare for the bad times just in case your fortune changes.

166

Control your mind and remain undisturbed.
That is the secret of Perfect Peace.
Sai Baba

Stress originates in your mind. The secret to remaining calm is to control your mind and not let anything disturb you. This sounds simple, but it takes a lot of discipline to maintain control over your mind. This is another part of a warrior's life that takes constant practice to perfect. Meditation is a vital part of maintaining a peaceful mind. Meditation calms your mind and gives you a sense of peace.

A technique that the warrior can use to maintain a calm mind, no matter what the circumstances are, is to do the best that you can do in every situation. If you have done all that you can possibly do, then that is all you can do. There is no need to get stressed out about any situation, because you know in your heart, that you have done everything in your power to take care of the problem. Thinking like this slows your mind down and gets to the very heart of the matter. You have done the best that you can do.

There is nothing else that you can do, so no matter what happens, you have done all that could be done. Once you have done your best, let the chips fall where they may. This doesn't mean that you don't continue to act as the circumstances continue to change. You continue to do all that you can do, and don't focus on what may happen, but just know that whatever happens, you will address it as it happens. Remain calm and think rationally. Don't allow things to get inside your head. Control your mind. Don't allow your emotions to take over. Think rationally and maintain your calm, peaceful mind.

167

Never walk away from home ahead of your axe and sword. You can't feel a battle in your bones or foresee a fight.
The Havamal

You really never know when you will have to defend yourself, especially when you are away from home. The Viking book of wisdom, *The Havamal*, tells us that you should never leave your axe and sword behind when you leave the security of your home. This means that you shouldn't leave home without being prepared to defend yourself. No one can foretell if they will be attacked or mugged when they are out and about. You have to be ready.

The way things seem to go, most people aren't attacked on the street when they are feeling pumped up and ready for anything that may happen. It seems that most attacks happen when people are least expecting something to happen or when they are sick and tired and don't feel like dealing with problems. You just never know. This is why you have to be aware and be prepared at all times, not just when you feel powerful and ready for some punk to cross your path.

Always be aware. Don't let your guard down. Don't get in such a hurry running around trying to complete your "to do" list that you become oblivious to everything around you. It is easy to allow your mind to become preoccupied when you are busy or when you have a ton of things to get done. Being aware and observant can save you much more time in the long run than all the rushing from place to place. A few minutes is a small price to pay for your safety and security.

168

Reputation often spills less blood.
Samurai Maxim

This samurai maxim appears to be in direct opposition to the teaching that you should conceal your weapons and your abilities, but it contains truth nonetheless. There is a time and a place for everything. There are times when concealing your skills is the wise thing to do, and yet at other times it may be wise to put your reputation to use, if you have a reputation as the samurai did.

The samurai had a reputation of being great warriors who could be fierce and deadly if the situation called for it. They were known as expert swordsmen. This reputation probably saved the lives of many men during the time of the samurai. Men who may have challenged an ordinary man over some trivial offense wouldn't consider challenging a samurai over the same transgression. Therefore, the samurai's reputation saved these men's lives, considering if they had challenged the samurai, they would have probably been killed.

The same notion can be true today, but you have to be very careful when it comes to counting on your reputation. Your reputation can help you resolve escalating conflicts, but having a reputation can also backfire on you. Your enemy may be so intimidated by your reputation that he is tempted to go to extremes in order to defeat you. We live in a different world than the samurai. Today someone may take a shot at you from across the street instead of confronting you face to face. In whatever situation you may find yourself, judgment is vital. Think before you speak or act.

168

Wisdom is not in words;
it is in understanding.
Hazrat Inayat Khan

Wisdom can be defined as the ability to make sensible decisions and judgments based on personal knowledge and experience. Wisdom is not in words, but rather in the personal knowledge that comes from understanding the words of wisdom which you read. Personal knowledge means that you have meditated and studied those words until they have become a part of you. This doesn't happen simply by reading through something; it takes attention and thought to transform these teachings into something useful.

Personal knowledge is only one part of obtaining wisdom according to this definition. The second part is personal experience. Experience comes from being actively involved or exposed to certain events or people. You can't get experience from reading a book; you get experience from participating in the world around you. You can get personal knowledge from a book, but to completely make wisdom your own, you need to combine that knowledge with experience.

This doesn't mean that you have to go out and make all the mistakes yourself in order to gain wisdom. Experience can be gained by observing the actions and behavior of others in relation to the personal knowledge that you have learned from those who have put their wisdom in writing. Be observant and look for ways in which you can turn the words of wisdom into your own personal understanding of wisdom. Learn from every experience, as well as the experiences of others. Only then will true wisdom be yours.

IF

If you can keep your head when all about you
Are losing theirs and blaming it on you;
If you can trust yourself when all men doubt you,
But make allowance for their doubting too;

If you can wait and not be tired by waiting,
Or, being lied about, don't deal in lies,
Or, being hated, don't give way to hating,
And yet don't look too good, nor talk too wise;

If you can dream - and not make dreams your master;
If you can think - and not make thoughts your aim;
If you can meet with triumph and disaster
And treat those two impostors just the same;

If you can bear to hear the truth you've spoken
Twisted by knaves to make a trap for fools,
Or watch the things you gave your life to broken,
And stoop and build 'em up with worn-out tools;

If you can make one heap of all your winnings
And risk it on one turn of pitch-and-toss,
And lose, and start again at your beginnings
And never breathe a word about your loss;

If you can force your heart and nerve and sinew
To serve your turn long after they are gone,
And so hold on when there is nothing in you
Except the Will which says to them: "Hold on!"

If you can talk with crowds and keep your virtue,
Or walk with kings - nor lose the common touch;
If neither foes nor loving friends can hurt you;
If all men count with you, but none too much;

If you can fill the unforgiving minute
With sixty seconds' worth of distance run -
Yours is the Earth and everything that's in it,
And - which is more - you'll be a Man, my son!

Rudyard Kipling

Afterword

Thank you for your purchase of *Warrior: The Way of Warriorhood*. I hope that you found the wisdom contained within to be useful in your life and for your goals as you travel along the path of the warrior. Please remember, that for this wisdom to truly become a part of who you are, you have to internalize it, meditate on it and keep it fresh in your mind. Wise words are only concepts. You must go beyond the concepts and actually experience the effects of the wisdom in your life.

I sincerely hope that you refer back to this book, as well as the other books in the *Warrior Wisdom series*, often and continue to meditate on the guidance provided by the many wise words it contains. Simply reading through this book once is not enough to make the wisdom it contains yours; you have to go past the reading, to a place of deep understanding for the wisdom to actually be useful. It is the fruits of the warrior lifestyle that are important, not the philosophy itself. All you learn and all you read is of little use to you if it doesn't produce real changes in your life.

Theodore Parker stated, "The books that help you most are those which make you think the most." I hope that *Warrior: The Way of Warriorhood* , has helped you abundantly. Hopefully, it has made you think about how you should live your life and the benefits of living the warrior lifestyle.

I would love to hear your feedback on Warrior Wisdom. What do you feel about what you have read? Did you find it helpful? Please send your comments on this, or any of the books in the Warrior Wisdom series, to me. You may contact me by e-mail at: **WarriorWisdom@comcast.net**, please put "Feedback" in the heading.

Live with honor!

Bohdi Sanders, Ph.D.

Appendix

Aeschylus – (525 BC–455 BC), ancient Greek playwright.

Aristotle – (384 BC–322 BC), Greek philosopher, a student of Plato and Teacher of Alexander the Great.

Aurelius, Marcus – (121–180), was Roman Emperor from 161 to his death in 180. He was the last of the "Five Good Emperors," and is also considered one of the most important Stoic philosophers.

Baba, Sai – South Indian guru, religious leader, orator.

Basho – (1644–1694), the most famous poet of the Edo period in Japan.

Beecher, Henry Ward – (1813–1887), was theologically liberal American Congregationalist clergyman and reformer, and author.

Bhagavad Gita – An ancient Sanskrit text.

Blake, William – (1757–1827), was an English poet, painter, printmaker, and essayist.

Bodhidharma – Buddhist monk said to spread the martial arts.

Buddha – (563 BC–483 BC), spiritual teacher from ancient India and the founder of Buddhism.

Byrhhe, Anne – (1906–1981), Norwegian writer.

Cao, Cao – (155–220), Chinese military leader and dictator.

Cardinal de Retz – (1614–1679), French churchman and writer.

Cervantes, Miguel de – (1547–1616), was a Spanish novelist, poet, and playwright. Cervantes is the author of *Don Quixote.*

Chief John Ross – (1790–1866), Chief of the Cherokee nation.

Chu, F. J. – Martial artist and author of "The Martial Way and its Virtues."

Chung Yung – is both a concept and one of the books of Neo Confucian teachings.

Cleveland, Harland – former US Ambassador to NATO.

Code of the Samurai – A Modern Translation of the Bushido Shoshinshu.

Confucius – (551 BC–479 BC), Chinese thinker and social philosopher, whose teachings and philosophy have deeply influenced Chinese, Korean, Japanese, and Vietnamese thought and life.

Dairai, Tomida – Confucian writer during the 1800's.

Democritus – (460 BC–370 BC), pre-Socratic Greek philosopher.

Deshimaru, Taisen – (1914–1982), Japanese Soto Zen Buddhist teacher. Born in the Saga Prefecture of Kyushu.

Dhammapada – is a Buddhist scripture, containing 423 verses in 26 categories. According to tradition, these are verses spoken by the Buddha on various occasions, most of which deal with ethics.

Einstein, Albert – (1879–1955), German-American physicist. He is best known for his Special and General Theories of Relativity.

Eliot, T.S. – (1888–1965), was an American-born English poet, dramatist and literary.

Emerson, Ralph Waldo – (1803–1882), American essayist, philosopher, poet, and leader of the Transcendentalist movement in the early 19th century.

Emperor Wen Di – Chinese emperor from 179 BC–157 BC.

Epictetus – (55–135), Greek Stoic philosopher.

Franklin, Benjamin – (1706–1790), was an American inventor, journalist, printer, diplomat, and statesman.

Funakoshi, Gichin – (1868–1957), founder of Shotokan karate and is attributed as being the "father of modern karate."

Furuya, Kensho – Martial artist, chief instructor of the Aikido Center In Los Angeles.

Gibran, Kahlil – (1883–1931), artist, poet and writer.

Gracian, Baltasar – (1601–1658), Spanish Baroque prose writer.

Hagakure – Japanese text for the warrior, drawn from a collection of commentaries by the samurai, Yamamoto Tsunetomo.

Harada, Mitsusuke – Japanese Karate master, founder of the Karate Do Shotokai.

Hatsumi, Masaaki – Founder and current head of the Bujinkan Dojo martial arts organization.

Havamal – Ancient Viking text.

Heckler, Richard Strozzi – Martial artist and author.

Heraclitus – (535 BC–475 BC), Greek philosopher.

Herodotus – (484 BC–425 BC), historian known for his writings on the Conflict between Greece and Persia.

Hitopadesa – Ancient Sanskrit text.

Homer – 7th century legendary ancient Greek poet.

Howard, Vernon – (1918–1992), American writer and spiritual teacher.

James, William – (1842–1910), pioneering American psychologist and philosopher.

Kant, Immanuel – (1724–1804), Prussian philosopher.

Karr, Alphonse – 1808–1890, French critic, journalist and novelist.

Khan, Hazrat Inayat – Sufi teacher and spiritualist.

Kipling, Rudyard – (1865–1936), British author and poet, born in India. In 1907, he was awarded the Nobel Prize for Literature, making him the first English language writer to receive the prize.

Kleiser, Grenville – (1868–1953), popular writer.

Lee, Bruce – (1940–1973), American-born martial artist, philosopher, instructor, martial arts actor and the founder of the Jeet Kune Do martial arts system.

Lieh Tzu, – 4th century Taoist scripture.

Lippmann, Walter – (1889–1974), influential United States writer, journalist, and political commentator.

Lord Chesterfield – (1694–1773), was a British statesman.

Malstrom, Bud – Martial artist and author.

Mann, Thomas – (1875–1955), German novelist, short story writer, Social critic, philanthropist, essayist, and 1929 Nobel Prize laureate.

Masters of Huainan – Ancient Taoist writing.

Miyagi, Gojun – Japanese martial artist.

Morgan, Forrest E. – Martial artist and author of *Living the Martial Way*.

Munenori, Yagyu Tajimanokami – Martial arts master.

Musashi, Miyamoto – (1584–1645), Japanese swordsman famed for his duels and distinctive style.

Nagauji, Hojo – Chief of the Kyoto agency in the 1300's.

Oxenham, John – (1852–1941), English journalist, novelist and poet.

Oyama, Masutatsu – (1923–1994), Karate master who founded Kyokushinkai, arguably the first and most influential style of full contact karate.

Parker, Ed – founder of American Kenpo.

Patton, George S. – (1885–1945), was a U.S. General during World War II; he was known in his time as "America's Fighting General."

Phaedrus – (15 BC–AD 50), Roman fabulist.

Rodin, Auguste – (1840–1917), French sculptor.

Roosevelt, Theodore – (1858–1919), also known as T.R. or Teddy, was the 26th President of the United States.

Rumi – (1207–1273), 13th century Persian poet, Islamic jurist, and theologian.

Sanders, Bohdi – Author, teacher, and martial artist.

Seabury, David – (1885–1960), American psychologist, author, and lecturer.

Seizen, Matsura – (1646–1713), martial artist, teacher and swordsman.

Shigetoki, Hojo – (1198–1261), Japanese samurai of the Kamakura period.

Shu Ching – Chinese classic, also known as the *Book of History.*

Sitting Bull – (1831–1890), was a Lakota Sioux holy man and war chief, defeated George Armstrong Custer at the Battle of the Little Big Horn.

Skinner, Dirk – Martial artist and author of *"Street Ninja."*

Sophocles – (496 BC–406 BC), ancient Greek playwright, dramatist, priest, and politician of Athens.

Suzuki, Daisetsu – (1870–1966), Buddhist writer.

Swami Sivananda – (1887–1963), Hindu spiritual teacher.

Tecumseh – (1768–1813), famous Shawnee leader. He spent much of his life attempting to rally disparate Native American tribes in a mutual defense of their lands, which eventually led to his death in the War of 1812.

Tiruvalluvar – 2nd century BC Tamil poet who wrote the Thirukkural, a well-known ethical work in Tamil literature.

Tohei, Koichi – 10th Dan Aikidoka and founder of the Ki Society and its style of Aikido.

Toju, Nakae – Confucian writer during the 1600's.

Totsudo, Saito – Confucian writer during the 1800's.

Tsuruoka, Masami – Martial arts master.

Tzu, Chuang – (369 BC–286 BC), literally *Master Zhuang*, was a Chinese philosopher, who is supposed to have lived during the Warring States Period.

Tzu, Hsun – (312 BC-235 BC), one of the important early Confucian philosophers.

Tzu, Lao – 6th century BC philosopher of ancient China and is a central figure in Taoism.

Tzu, Sun – (544 BC–496 BC), the author of *The Art of War*, an immensely influential ancient Chinese book on military strategy.

Van Fleet, James – (1892-1992), American military general.

Voltaire – (1694-1778), French writer, deist and philosopher.

Von Goeth, Johann Wolfgang – (1749–1832), German novelist, dramatist, poet, humanist, scientist, and philosopher.

Washington, George – (1732–1799), the first President of the United States, and leader of the Continental Army during the American Revolutionary War.

Worden, Kelly S. – Martial artist and author.

Xunzi – (310 BC–220 BC), Chinese political philosopher.

Yoda – Jedi master from the Star Wars films.

Yoshimasa, Shiba – 12th century samurai.

WARRIOR WISDOM

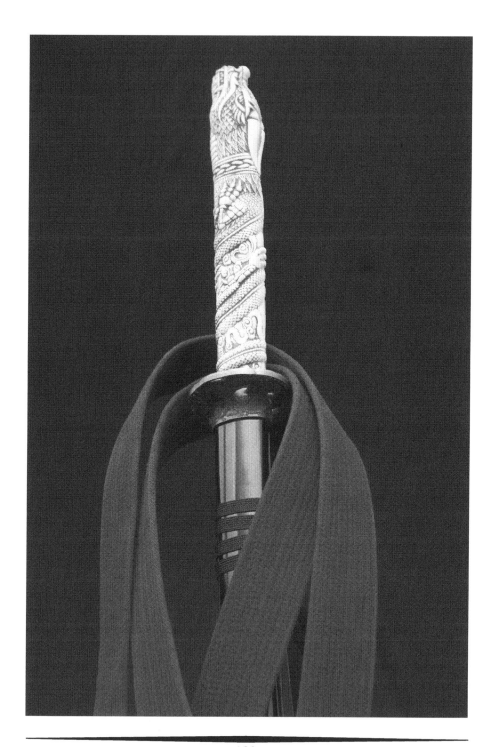

Index

Other Titles by Bohdi Sanders

Character! Honor! Integrity! Are these traits that guide your life and actions? *Warrior Wisdom: Ageless Wisdom for the Modern Warrior* focuses on how to live your life with character, honor and integrity. This book is highly acclaimed, has won multiple awards and is endorsed by some of the biggest names in martial arts and the world of self-help. *Warrior Wisdom* is filled with wise quotes and useful information for anyone who strives to live a life of excellence. This book will help you live your life to the fullest!

Secrets of the Soul is a guide to uncovering your deeply hiden beliefs. This delightful book provides over 1,150 probing questions which guide you to a thorough understanding of who you are and what you believe. Take this unbelievably entertaining journey to a much deeper place of self-awareness. Where do your beliefs come from? Do you really know exactly what you believe and why you believe it? You will after reading *Secrets of the Soul*. This book will help you uncover your true beliefs!

The Warrior Lifestyle is the last installment of the award winning *Warrior Wisdom Series*. Forwarded by martial arts legend Loren W. Christensen, this book has been dubbed as highly inspirational and motivational. If you want to live your life to the fullest, you need to read this one! Don't settle for an ordinary life, make your life extraordinary! The advice and wisdom shines on every page of this book, making it a must read for everyone who strives to live an extraordinary life of character and honor!

Other Titles by Bohdi Sanders

Wisdom of the Elders is a unique, one-of-a-kind quote book. This book is filled with quotes that focus on living life to the fullest with honor, character, and integrity. Honored by the USA Book News with a 1st place award for Best Books of the Year in 2010, this book is a guide for life. *Wisdom of the Elders* contains over 4,800 quotes, all which lead the reader to a life of excellence. If you enjoy quotes, wisdom, and knowledge, you will love this book. This is truly the ultimate quote book for those searching for wisdom!

Defensive Living takes the reader deep into the minds of nine of the most revered masters of worldly wisdom. It reveals valuable insights concerning human nature from some of the greatest minds the world has ever known, such as Sun Tzu, Gracian, Goethe, and others. *Defensive Living* presents invaluable lessons for living and advice for avoiding the many pitfalls of human relationships. This is an invaluable and entertaining guidebook for living a successful and rewarding life!

Modern Bushido is all about living a life of excellence. This book covers 30 essential traits that will change your life. *Modern Bushido* expands on the standards and principles needed for a life of excellence, and applies them directly to life in today's world. Readers will be motivated and inspired by the straightforward wisdom in this enlightening book. If you want to live a life of excellence, this book is for you! This is a must read for every martial artist and anyone who seeks to live life as it is meant to be lived.

MODERN BUSHIDO
Living a Life of Excellence

Modern Bushido

Living a Life of Excellence

Modern Bushido: Living a Life of Excellence is all about living a life of excellence. This enlightening new book covers 30 essential traits that will change your life, and which are vital to living the warrior lifestyle.

In *Modern Bushido* you will learn:

- How to live a life of character
- How your thoughts affect your life
- What it means to be a true friend
- Why discipline is vital in your life
- How to live a life of excellence
- What self-defense *really* means
- How to be a peace with death
- Why you should be courteous
- What true courage is
- The true meaning of honor
- The benefits of meditation
- Why sincerity is important
- What true respect means
- Your ultimate responsibility
- How to balance your life
- And much, much more…

Modern Bushido provides you with a complete overview of the essential traits which build a life of excellence. It provides you with a multitude of life-changing analogies, quotes, life lessons, guidance, and soul-searching questions of value and ethics.

You will be motivated and inspired by the straightforward lessons of wisdom and honor in this book. If you want to live a life of excellence, this book is for you!

A MUST READ for all martial artists and everyone who strives to live a life of honor and integrity!

Order Your Copy Today!

Looking for More Wisdom?

If you are interested in living the warrior lifestyle or simply in living a life of character, integrity and honor you will enjoy The Wisdom Warrior website and newsletter. The Wisdom Warrior website contains dozens of articles, useful links, and news for those seeking to live the warrior lifestyle.

The newsletter is also a valuable resource. Each edition of The Wisdom Warrior Newsletter is packed with motivating quotes, articles, and information which everyone will find useful in their journey to perfect their character and live the life which they were meant to live.

The Wisdom Warrior Newsletter is a newsletter sent directly to your email account and is absolutely FREE! There is no cost or obligation to you whatsoever. You will also receive the current news updates and new articles by Dr. Bohdi Sanders as soon as they are available. Your email address is never shared with anyone else.

All you need to do to start receiving this valuable and informative newsletter is to go to the Wisdom Warrior website and simply sign up. It is that simple! You will find The Wisdom Warrior website at:

www.TheWisdomWarrior.com

Also, be sure to find posts by Dr. Sanders on Facebook. Dr. Sanders posts enlightening commentaries, photographs, and quotes throughout the week on his Facebook pages. You can find them at:

www.facebook.com/The.Warrior.Lifestyle

www.facebook.com/EldersWisdom

www.facebook.com/bohdi.sanders

Don't miss the opportunity to receive tons of FREE wisdom, enlightening posts, interesting articles, and intriguing photographs on The Wisdom Warrior website and on Dr. Sanders' Facebook pages.

Sign Up Today!

31974406R00121

Made in the USA
Lexington, KY
02 May 2014